THE
Experiential
Learning Toolkit

BLENDING PRACTICE
WITH CONCEPTS

COLIN BEARD

KoganPage

LONDON PHILADELPHIA NEW DELHI

Publisher's note

Every possible effort has been made to ensure that the information contained in this book is accurate at the time of going to press, and the publishers and author cannot accept responsibility for any errors or omissions, however caused. No responsibility for loss or damage occasioned to any person acting, or refraining from action, as a result of the material in this publication can be accepted by the editor, the publisher or the author.

First published in Great Britain and the United States in 2010 by Kogan Page Limited

120 Pentonville Road	525 South 4th Street, #241	4737/23 Ansari Road
London N1 9JN	Philadelphia PA 19147	Daryaganj
United Kingdom	USA	New Delhi 110002
www.koganpage.com		India

© Colin Beard, 2010

The right of Colin Beard to be identified as the author of this work has been asserted by him in accordance with the Copyright, Designs and Patents Act 1988.

ISBN   978 0 7494 5078 6
E-ISBN 978 0 7494 5934 5

British Library Cataloguing-in-Publication Data

A CIP record for this book is available from the British Library.

Library of Congress Cataloging-in-Publication Data

Beard, Colin (Colin M.)
  The experiential learning toolkit : blending practice with concepts / Colin Beard.
    p. cm.
  ISBN 978-0-7494-5078-6 – ISBN 978-0-7494-5934-5 (ebook)   1. Experiential learning.
2. Active learning. 3. Employees–Training of.   I. Title.

  BF318.5.B427 2010
  153.1'52–dc22
                              2010006391

Typeset by Saxon Graphics Ltd, Derby
Printed and bound in India by Replika Press Pvt Ltd

Contents

Figures and tables

Figures

Tables

Preface

In this book I present a milieu of experiential ways to learn: either on our own or with other people. My thinking behind these experiences are the result of both my own life journeys and the thinking and interactions with many other people that I have had the pleasure of working with throughout the world. Meeting such people and interacting with them has been fascinating and a very enjoyable part of my own learning journey. At this stage however I would like to say that what I offer here in this book is presented in the spirit of sharing and exchanging.

My own adventures in life, my experiential field, have impacted upon me considerably, particularly the period whilst studying zoology as a student when I organized a three month wildlife expedition to the Amazon jungle in 1975 after my formal studies ended. My zoological schooling in morphology, that is the observation of living things, particularly in terms of their form and structure, will be apparent in many experiential activities that are offered in this book I am sure. Other significant life adventures have included getting lost in the Malaysian jungles, and living in a very hot, wooden garden shed during the worst recorded summer drought in UK history whilst looking after the red kite, which was then a rare bird of prey reduced to a mere twenty seven pairs and confined to a specific area of mid-Wales. Another noteworthy job involved spending many hours each day in a boat (or stranded during low tide on mud flats) in my role to protect sea birds for the Royal Society for the Protection of Birds in Langstone Harbour, near Portsmouth. I learnt to handle boats the experiential way! Later I also learnt the rudiments of many practical skills such as fencing, walling, hedge laying and tree felling during my time working for the British Trust for Conservation Volunteers. I learnt campaigning skills, planning regulations, speaking in public enquiries, land management and wildlife protection skills whilst working for a variety of other wildlife charities. I have taught in schools, and I now teach in higher education and lecture in Sheffield Business School. I continue to develop my interest in learning beyond the classroom and some years ago I set up a new Master's degree in Outdoor Management Development. As well as being an employee working in higher education I simultaneously posses self-employed status, generating consultancy work with many interesting people in both large and small organizations around the globe. These life events are my own experiential platform, for my own adult learning. These experiences clearly affect the way I now think and work.

This varied backcloth of life experience with voluntary, private and public organizations has considerably widened my horizon leading to the creation of my values and principles about working and learning with people, and with 'nature'. As I progress in life I know that the business of learning is very much part of me, and my sense of who I am, my identity and my 'being'. However over the last twenty five years I have also begun to feel that my exploration of 'experiential learning' has really only just begun, and that I have only really scratched the surface of what is out there. For sure I have already learnt a great deal but I want to continue to find out so much more. No doubt I will certainly continue to reframe and re-think my thinking about experiential learning: it is a complex subject that has a lineage embedded in many philosophies about human life. Learning is concerned with the very process of being and becoming in the world.

Throughout the book the term 'learning experience' will be mostly but not exclusively used, rather than activity. 'Learning experiences', whether they are created by learners, facilitators, educators or trainers, or indeed anyone who wants to understand and work with their own or others learning, are the core of this book. In writing this book I am very conscious of the fact that in mediating learning experiences in varying ways there is a diminishing boundaries between teacher and learner, and I know that when I am involved in education, training or in the development of others, I do learning so much from the experience. The role of learner and facilitator are variously interchangeable. Indeed my view is that a great deal can be learnt by 'teaching' others, and a maxim I use when working with corporate trainers is '*Let the learners do the learning*': some trainers exhaust themselves telling people the corporate message, or the answers to problems, playing sage on the stage. There is always something new to learn and when we engage in critical reflection on or in our own teaching or training practice, we become better learners.

An experiential learning model that I created in 2002 was presented in a co-authored text with my colleague and friend John Wilson. My thinking about this model has continued to mature, and so it has changed since that time. I have worked on it and continue to try to find both time and money to research areas of this 'whole person' approach to learning and I continue to struggle to describe terms such as *belonging* and *being*.

The experiential ideas and activities I present in this book all have a theoretical base to them and much of the underpinning research I have undertaken with many colleagues has been published in a wide variety of scholarly and professional journals. These include a diverse range of subject areas as illustrated in the sample below.

- British Educational Research Journal;
- *European Business Review;*
- *Industrial and Commercial Training;*
- *Environmental Management and Health;*
- *International Journal of Facilities Management;*
- *Australian Journal of Outdoor Education;*
- *Journal of Town and Country Planning;*
- *Sustainable Product Design;*
- *Teaching in Higher Education;*
- *Journal of the Institute of Public Rights of Way;*
- *Leisure and Tourism Research;*
- *Journal of Leisure, Hospitality, Sport and Tourism Education;*
- *Environmental Training in Engineering Education;*
- *Eco-Management and Auditing;*
- *Leisure Manager* – Leisure Industries;
- *People Management* – CIPD;
- *Horizons* – Outdoor Learning;
- *Times Higher.*

The learning experiences offered in this book have also been tried and tested with very large numbers of people, from an extensive range of cultures and within many situated contexts – from education, to corporate training and to individual and organizational development. These testing grounds, and the rich milieu of people involved, have included such locations as Ireland, Finland, Czech Republic, Singapore, Dubai and Sharjah in Middle East, Nairobi in Africa, Malaysia, India, Taiwan, Hong Kong, Australia and mainland China.

Acknowledgements

Many people have encouraged me to develop my thinking about learning and development, and to put my thoughts in writing. My wife Maggie has supported me continuously in this journey. I have also received much support from my friends and colleagues, and in particular I would like to thank Pratik Palan, owner of Evoexl Learning Solutions. He has been a great friend and companion during my work in India and the Asian region. I am also indebted to the support given by Yan Hongliang, companion and friend on my travels across China. Thanks also go to my friends Tan Ming Yen and Eric Lai have also connected me to many learning opportunities across China and Taiwan; to Joni Ong, Abdul Kahlid and Jeffrey Chua in Singapore and to Chin Yook Kong in Malaysia. Over many years I have had the benefit of much wisdom and humour from Helen Hirst, Deputy Chief Executive of Bradford and Airedale PCT.

Introduction

Not just another 50 activities!

The majority of books on experiential learning are either practical or theoretical. In this book the practical ideas are connected to essential theory. The book is written for practitioners, and practice is illustrated through a wide range of 'experiences' that are presented as material for learning.

Thirty experiences are presented and they cover a wide range of topics, from service learning and corporate social responsibility to customer service skills, telephone skills and company product knowledge retention. Advanced skills for higher levels of strategic thinking and negotiating are also included, as well as financial skills, time management and the development of innovation and creativity. These learning experiences are presented as if they are mediated by a trainer or educator. However, some experiences are taken from typical everyday-life situations so that they can form the basis of unmediated learning. In most cases there are opportunities to critically explore multiple meanings of the learning experience, both from a personal perspective and from the meanings constructed by other people. The interpretations that result thus arise from numerous perspectives and contexts (see, for example, Chapter 1.1: Just four steps, and Chapter 5.5: Walk the talk).

All the experiences are detailed so as to make key links to fundamental theoretical concepts. The experiences can be located within both indoor and outdoor contexts, and they cover a range of professional sectors. Furthermore the book can be used alongside the companion text, *Experiential Learning: A Best Practice Handbook for Educators and Trainers* by Colin Beard and John P Wilson, first published in 2002 and later substantially rewritten almost as a completely new text (Kogan Page, 2006).

An overarching model

Many writers have concerned themselves with experiential learning, whole-person learning and adult learning. All have investigated aspects of the experience of learning to differing degrees: the result is that there is contention over what dimensions are considered important. The controversy continues about the extent to which learning is socially (with other people), psychologically (inner psyche/self), emotionally (feelings), cognitively (thinking) or otherwise created. This book will integrate six of these important dimensions, as they are considered the foundations of any learning experience.

In order to connect the six chosen dimensions, an overarching model, first presented in previous books (Beard in Beard and Wilson, 2002, 2006) will be applied to facilitate the exploration and understanding of these important dimensions of learning, as located within a range of essential theories. While the model is merely a structure, the thinking behind the model is substantially grounded in practice: the model initially emerged by asking six basic questions about the nature of the experience of learning. These are: 1) where did the learning take place? (working with the learning environment); 2) what kind of learning activities were engaged with? (the 'what' of learning); 3) how were the senses engaged in the experience? (the 'how' of learning); 4) in what way was there emotional engagement? (the 'heart' in learning); 5) how were intelligence and knowledge applied? (the 'mind' of learning); and 6) in what way did personal change occur? (the change dimension). Practitioner work on these six questions underlies the core idea behind this workbook, and so the book is simply divided according to these same six sections.

Each section of the book will focus, albeit artificially, on one single learning dimension at a time, and within each dimension several underpinning concepts will be explained. The six dimensions are of course all artificially separated. In reality all are inextricably interwoven.

Learning through imaginative 'experiences'

All the experiences described in the book can of course be altered to suit differing contexts, circumstances, preferences and conditions. The layout of the book means that it is easy to dip into, rather than necessarily being read from front to back. There are many books with titles such as 'Fifty activities to improve your training' or 'One hundred and one team-building activities for...' or 'Five hundred of the best corporate activities...'. This book has not been created to be just another off-the-shelf approach to experiential design; rather, the selected activities are presented and detailed so as to illustrate a set of central principles that might open up, rather than reduce down, the possibilities for experiential learning. To use a food metaphor, if the taste, texture and presentation of food are understood and appreciated, then immeasurable new recipes can be created.

Off-the-shelf packages present something that is repeatable; such books can create a dependency, requiring little more than an ability to reproduce a set recipe for the learning experience. They can also become 'well trodden'. A typical example of a popular learning experience is the 'Spider's web' used in outdoor learning. This is a team-building activity that uses a network of strings or ropes strung between two trees so as to create a web-like rope structure. The web is usually constructed so it has enough openings for each team member to fit through. The team has to get all its people through these spaces without touching the string or ropes. Of course, getting the last person through requires some innovative thinking. This activity has, however, been applied to ever lower age groups, with the result that it can turn out to be uncomfortable when corporate executives, expecting new challenging team activities, unexpectedly remark 'I remember doing this at school!' Set activities can unfortunately have the potential to be experienced as 'out of the can'. One experienced colleague working in outdoor learning and adventure termed these 'adventure in a bun'!

Fast-food-type experiences are often used for learning, and so the art of cooking is eventually lost. This is counter to the philosophy of this book. The underpinning conceptual thinking behind all the experiences presented in this book is made clear so it can be understood and linked to future explorations of practice. This will hopefully allow alternative, tailor-made experiences to be created for personal and organizational learning.

Models: their strengths and weaknesses

The overarching model that this book is based on might, like other models, be criticized as presenting formulaic interpretations of complex human life: after all, humans are not predictable machines. Furthermore, designing activities according to a set model or formula can be argued to be mere gimmick or technique. Experiential learning cannot be reduced to set strategies, formulas or recipes. Working with people, and their inherent complexity, is certainly not easy. The reason that models and frameworks are presented here is not to provide answers, but to support, to help people get started, to show how to work with, and to navigate through, some of the complexity of human learning experiences. In reality, separation of these six dimensions is of course artificial. The London Underground map is also an artificial representation of reality. Yet this colour-coded model helps large numbers of people to navigate the sizeable city of London. Once the city is known, the map may not be needed: everyday learning from experience in due course can make such guiding maps and models redundant. However, it is important to remember that maps and models not only open up new vistas; they can also constrain thinking.

Contemporary issues: emotions and learning

Whether in management education, corporate training, youth development work, higher education or learning in schools, our understanding of the experience of learning is continually developing and changing. Many contemporary writers on learning describe how their own thinking continues to evolve and be reformulated. In 2001 John Heron voiced concern that 'The old model of education, going back to classical times, dealt only with the education of the intellect, theoretical and applied.' Heron developed an integrative model linking the emotional, the interpersonal and the political dimensions of learning. Significantly he remarked that 'Nowadays we have people who are learning by thinking, feeling and doing – bringing all these to bear on the acquisition of new knowledge and skills' (Heron, 2001: 208). Heron thus highlighted the importance of three dimensions of learning.

The 'feeling' dimension of learning now receives renewed interest, and well-known authors on adult education have added a new focus to this dimension. In 2006 Peter Jarvis acknowledged that emotions were more significant than he had imagined in earlier work. Similarly, Knud Illeris published *The Three Dimensions of Learning* in 2002 and added the role of emotion to his thinking about learning, and began to argue that learning involves three major core dimensions: cognition, emotion and society. Illeris noted that: 'In order for learning to be characterized as formation of experience, the learner must be actively present and be self-aware in his or her interaction with the social and/ or material environment' (2002: 157).

While thinking, feeling and doing, and social dynamics are important dimensions of learning, there are also other, equally significant, dimensions that are often omitted in whole-person theories. There is much variation in thinking as to the primacy of the social or the political or cultural contextual milieu. Views about the importance of emotions or the significance of the role of the body, or the impact of specific spaces on learning, including the natural world, all vary considerably. These important areas require further exploration.

Taking an integrative approach: connecting six core dimensions of learning

The overarching model of six dimensions is presented below. The model is robust and it has been subjected to considerable scrutiny including a doctoral submission, publication in refereed journals, and numerous other forms of academic and professional critique. It takes the visual form of a combination lock. Using this visual metaphor, a series of tumblers represent the six dimensions. The potential number of permutations that can be configured is infinite, but it is not designed to mechanistically create permutations. If you are not a fan of models and frameworks, then other metaphors might be more suitable. These six dimensions can be simply considered as six 'spaces', created for learners to work in. The six dimensions might represent balls that continually require to be 'juggled' in experiential learning practice.

The model in Figure 0.1, in its elementary sense, is based on the notion that the internal world of a learner interacts with the external environment through the senses. The theoretical position adopted by Illeris (2002) presents the social and societal dimensions as key in the external world, with the emotions and cognition key in the inner-world dimension of learning. This might be regarded as a socially over-determined interpretation of the outer-world experience, a position adopted by many who write on experiential learning and adult education. Outdoor learning, the outdoor environment and other significant spaces and places, including the natural world itself, receive little consideration. Living entities other than the human world are often denigrated to the status of the 'material world'. The social is seen as synonymous with 'the world'. The part played by the senses and the body in learning similarly receive little attention. This is understandable to an extent and might occur due to limitations in the experiential fields of the writers. Understandably they cannot experience first-hand the very varied field of practice.

Critical commentaries offer insight and a deeper appreciation of the limitations of theoretical arguments. For example, Payne (2002), an outdoor educator, suggests a reconciliation of the inner- and outer-world experiences as worthy of pursuit, particularly for critical outdoor learning. Payne suggests a 'sorely needed reparation of first, human-environment, second, community/society-land/sea/town/cityscapes, and, third, culture–nature relations' (2002: 19). It is with this in mind that the model outlined in Figure 0.1 is offered as a more comprehensive and integrative approach as Payne suggests.

The experience of learning has an outer-world element to it and the practical questions that we might usefully ask are:

1. Where, when and in what climate or social/political/environmental context is the learning taking place?
2. What kind of learning activity might be best suited for this person or group of people? Why is 'doing' regarded as important in experiential learning?

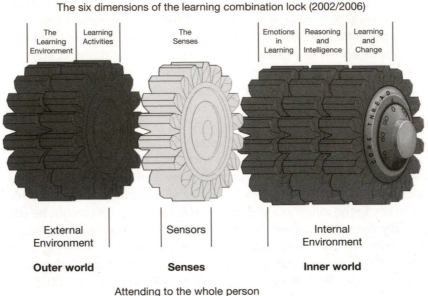

One Approach

The six dimensions of the learning combination lock (2002/2006)

| The Learning Environment | Learning Activities | The Senses | Emotions in Learning | Reasoning and Intelligence | Learning and Change |

| External Environment | Sensors | Internal Environment |

| **Outer world** | **Senses** | **Inner world** |

Attending to the whole person

Original version first presented by Beard in Beard and Wilson (2002)

Figure 0.1   *An overarching simple framework or model embracing six dimensions of the learning experience*

The outer-world experience is, however, connected to our inner world by the senses. The question then becomes:

3. How will the experience be internalized, received, by the senses (including the body) of the learner/s?

The inner world of the learner is where the experience is processed and questions might include:

4. What is the emotional impact of the experience?
5. How is the mind processing the experience? How is the mind stimulated and engaged? What thinking is taking place?
6. What kind of change or transformation, if any, is occurring?

These six questions exploring learning can be usefully asked by either the facilitator or the learner, as part of the process of reflection in and on learning. An important critical question of 'Why?' is also required, challenging 'Why is this being done?' This question should be continually applied across the six dimensions. Senge *et al* (1994) suggests using a continuous sequence of five Whys? to investigate practice at successively deeper levels, and to generate a more critical view.

Understanding concepts that connect theory and practice

The model has practical titles as well as six theoretical titles allocated to each of the six dimensions. This is in order to highlight the connectivity between practice and theory. The model simultaneously has practical simplicity and theoretical complexity. In Figure 0.1, both practical and theoretical titles are shown: practical titles are shown at the top and theoretical titles are shown at the bottom. The model thus links a theoretical interpretation (at the bottom) to the detail of everyday practice in the surface layer (at the top).

Beginning on the left of the model, the first dimension, shown as a tumbler, is the 'where', the environment or place and space that learning takes place, providing the location, external stimuli and ambience for the experience. There are of course many social, political, cultural (and spiritual) dynamics that exist in the outer-world experience. It is the 'where' of learning, where and in what context it is located. Thus it relates to the wider sense of being in the world, our sense of 'belonging'. Thus this dimension is going to be referred to as the 'belonging' dimension. Belonging in the world has considerable theoretical complexity: it forms the basis of much philosophical debate. In this dimension of learning, five practical experiences will be illustratively used to highlight the following conceptual areas: 1) bodily or kinaesthetic learning that uses space in a creative way; 2) reading and the creation of a relaxed but alert mind state, using quiet, private spaces; 3) immersive experiences in a new town or city spaces, resulting in an 'edventure', a combination of education and adventure that explores cultural, historical and other contextual experiences that create a new socio-spatial dynamic; 4) the spatial movement of information, exploring how it alters the 'view', through bodily sensory receptors (proprioception); here the relationships between forms of knowing such as everyday knowing and abstract knowing are explored; and 5) silence and solo experiences in specific environments.

The second tumbler represents the 'what': what are people going to do in order to learn? This dimension is about the milieu of possible learning activities that might involve building something or going on a physical journey or experiencing a mathematical challenge or solving a problem. This dimension is thus called the 'doing' dimension. In this section, five practical experiences will be illustratively used to highlight the following conceptual areas: 1) constructing and deconstructing within problem-based learning (PBL); 2) raising and lowering the degree of reality within an experience; 3) matching or analogous experiences, ie introducing people while learning how to write introductions; 4) a morphological 'reading' of material using observational skills and visual literacy; and 5) an auditory focus on voice analysis in order to explore sequence and flow, shape and form in learning experiences.

The third, fourth and fifth group of tumblers are concerned with the inner world. Starting with the 'how', the third tumbler represents the senses through which we receive the various forms of stimuli. This is thus called the 'sensing' dimension. In this section, five practical experiences will be illustratively used to highlight the following conceptual areas: 1) sensory work as used to understand, and learn about, a range of business products, and the senses used in contemporary brand development; 2) sensory reduction and visual blanking used in learning; 3) shape and colour as used for developing conversations about learning styles and personality characteristics; 4) stepped sensory stimulation, used to heighten levels of engagement in learning, and as used to develop intellectual engagement; and 5) somatosensory (bodily sense work) linked to visual acuity applied to organizing, sorting and classifying skills.

The fourth tumbler involves the emotions (the 'heart' of learning), where we perceive, interpret and emotionally respond to the stimuli from the external environment; in other words, we internalize the external learning experience. This is the 'feeling' dimension and connects with theories of affect or emotions. In this section, five practical experiences will be illustratively used to highlight the following conceptual areas: 1) using playing cards to access inner feelings and to establish the relationship between these feelings and other experiences of learning; 2) using metaphors to access underlying values and feelings; 3) the use of reframing to access and to rewrite inner-voice scripts; 4) using unfinished statements to create spaces to explore and reflect upon emotional experiences; and 5) using string to map a roller coaster of experiences and establish the roller-coaster relationships between positive and negative experiences.

The fifth tumbler focuses on the scope and form of intelligence and cognition (mind). This is referred to as the 'knowing' dimension. In this section, five practical experiences will be illustratively used to highlight the following conceptual areas: 1) the development of innovative minds through the exploration of linear and non-linear patterns; 2) vertical and lateral mapping to develop critical and conceptual thought; 3) a mathematical–logical deconstruction experience applied to problem-based learning (PBL); 4) understanding complexity through analogy and metaphor; and 5) using bodily movement, vocal reinforcement and spatial-relational awareness (proprioception) to understand complex information.

The final tumbler concerns the theories of learning and change. This is the 'becoming' dimension. It is referred to as the inner 'being' dimension and has underlying psychoanalytic theories of identity, associated with the inner self, and our ability and willingness to change and become someone. It is about knowing oneself. In this section five practical experiences will be illustratively used to highlight the following conceptual areas: 1) identifying personality traits and characteristics using reflective card-playing experiences; 2) visual self- and group reflections using digital media; 3) communication and behavioural awareness through sensitization; 4) learning through service to the community and environment; and 5) uncovering the inner self, altering persona, lowering reality of self, playfulness.

These six dimensions of the learning experience thus have layers of interpretation that can be either practical or theoretical. Oscillation between the practice questions and the deeper theoretical concepts will support the development of practical wisdom. As you read through the book, you may well see things occurring in practice and so it is possible to add to the concepts, and perhaps even develop completely new dimensions: the creation of a personalized version of the model is thus possible. This can encourage professional reflection, an exploration and critical examination of successes, obstacles and challenges.

At the very base of Table 0.1 the words form and formless are presented. They are concerned with experience as connected with the ego, and levels of consciousness. Form relates to very tangible experiences with both our ego and with things that are to do with what we get, want, have, do or know. These things are of the material world. Getting qualifications, getting a job relate to form. 'Doing' activities relate to form, and knowing about things relates to the form – of things. Formless relates to the deeper unconscious: of the inner self on the right, and of the (connected) outer formless world of spirit, and nature. Meditation, for example, is an experience that can lead to the understanding of the inner self: it is not concerned with the form of material things. These difficult concepts to grapple with are deliberately included here: there is an illustrative 'listening to silence' solo experience described in the belonging dimension of the book, and detailed discussion is included in chapters on spiritual work and natural intelligence and mind states in Beard and Wilson (2006). These matters of ego and the unconscious do present themselves in education and training experiences: they should not be ignored simply because they are difficult to understand and explain. A simple introduction to this complex area is the work of Eckhart Tolle (2005).

Gerard Egan in *The Skilled Helper* (2001: 19) talks about the common-sense wisdom in the helping professions and suggests that 'Helpers need to be wise, and part of their job is to impart some of their wisdom, however indirectly, to their clients.' He then says that a number of authors have defined wisdom as 'an expertise in the conduct and meaning of life' or 'an expert knowledge system concerning the fundamental pragmatics of life'. Developing a sense of inner being, and the desire to develop wisdom, are concerned with self-knowledge

Table 0.1   *The development of the model*

Connecting inner and outer worlds					
1 Outer world of learner		**2** Sensory interface	**3** Inner world of learner		
Developed into six practical dimensions					
1 Learning environment	**2** Learning activity	**3** Senses	**4** Affect – emotions	**5** Reason – mind	**6** Learning and change
Key practitioner questions to ask					
Where? Where, with whom and in what contextual circum-stances, does learning take place?	What? What will the learners actually do?	How? How will learners receive this experience?	Hearts? What is the nature of the emotional engagement?	Minds? What is the nature of the cognitive engagement?	Change? How can learners be encouraged to change?
Linking essential theory					
belonging	doing	sensing	feeling	thinking	being (and becoming)
potential to engage the less tangible – formless	focus on tangible things – form ←——————————————————————→				potential to engage the less tangible – formless

and maturity, knowledge of life's obligations and goals, and tolerance for ambiguity and the ability to work with it. They embrace holistic thinking and open-mindedness, contextual thinking and the ability to spot flaws in reasoning, to go with intuition, and the ability to synthesize. Significantly he suggests that wisdom is the refusal to let experience become a liability through the creation of blind spots. Wisdom is surely experience at its best with the ego denied the ability to get in the way of life values and difficult decisions.

Practical experience and the six dimensions

Through the continual refining of practice, more concepts will tend to arise within these six dimensions of learning. It becomes apparent that there are things that will support learning and things that create blockages or barriers to learning. Some important concepts within each learning dimension are shown in Table 0.2. They are presented as being illustrative.

Table 0.2 *The milieu of conceptual work that might emerge from each of the six dimensions*

BELONGING and the concepts of working with:	DOING and the concepts of working with:	SENSING and the concepts of working with:	FEELING and the concepts of working with:	KNOWING and the concepts of working with:	BEING and the concepts of working with:
Place	Doing	Body	Feeling	Ways of knowing	Transfer
Space	Real–simulated	Auditory	Fear/anxiety	Epistemological self	Reflection
Real–simulated	Rules–obstacles	Olfactory	Pride/shame	Multiple intelligence:	PPD
Indoor–outdoor	Collaborative	Visual: dark–light	Energy/tension	kinaesthetic/body,	Planned Emergent
Natural–artificial	Social–cultural	Silence	Fantasy	spatial, inter-/	Growth
Urban–rural	Competitive	Solitude and	Relationships	intra-personal,	Maturity
Situated	Edventure	presence	Body-emotion	mathematical	Self
Community	Journey–solo	Touch	Acceptance	Wisdom	Identity
Social and political	Planned–unplanned	S-enhancement	Rejection	Mind states,	Wisdom
dynamics	Narrow skills	S-reduction	Elation	meditation, flow	Spiritual
Physical learning	Broad skills	S-focusing	Ebullience	Psyche	Becoming someone
spaces	Research and	Visual literacy	Sadness–pleasure	Spiritual and	Consciousness
Silent spaces	problem-based doing	Colour	Transfer	naturalistic	Presence
E-spaces		Sensory intelligence	Projection	intelligence	
			Reframing		
			Transgression		

The conceptual themes can take many years of practice to understand: there are clearly many, many more to learn about, as the list is not in any way complete. Throughout the book the practical learning experiences will outline many of these concepts. Patience is a key ingredient in developing a commitment to developing as a reflective practitioner and a lifelong learner.

Exploring theoretical concepts

Learning experiences are offered in this book to generate insight into some of the core concepts of experiential learning as highlighted in Table 0.2. The 'higher' conceptual view is developed through an understanding of practice. The 'higher' thinking thus operates as linked to experience or activity. Two examples might best illustrate this point.

First, in the doing dimension of an experience, the obvious and important question is: doing what? In Table 0.2 this dimension of learning contains the word 'real'. This is a concept to be explored in terms of how the perception of the realness of the experience can be altered to the benefit of the learning experience. In experiential learning 'doing' has been equated with physical activity, and there are assumptions that 'doing the real thing' is best for learning: a core concept that needs to be questioned and further refined. By drilling down into the dimension of 'doing', and in particular the conceptual question of the value of doing the 'real' thing, experiential activities can be studied in practice so as to highlight examples where perceptions of realness can be lowered or raised to the advantage of learning. A practical example that explores this conceptual area, and which is found in the doing section of the book, is the experience of 'negotiating'. Here examples are given to illustrate how many elements of the experience alter the sense of reality. The five experiences covered in this dimension explore different types of 'doing'. They are: 1) 'doing' as in constructing and problem solving objects; 2) 'doing' as in negotiating with people; 3) 'doing' as in writing; 4) 'doing' as in observation and description; and 5) 'doing' as in talking.

For a second example, let us take another dimension, that of the sensing dimension of learning. The key role of the senses in learning has been recognized by many great thinkers, from Aristotle onwards. Aristotle considered that there was nothing in the intellect that did not first exist in the senses. This important role for the senses is acknowledged in outdoor learning, where the practice of using blindfolds is prevalent. Frequent use of blindfolds can reduce thinking to a rudimentary level: blindfolds prevent people from seeing. A higher or more conceptual interpretation might involve working with the senses, in order to explore how they affect learning. By changing the language used, from blindfold to sensory intelligence, the mind is opened up to new possibilities: it moves beyond blindfolds (and out-of-the-can usage), generating concepts such as 'sensory reduction', 'sensory enhancement', 'sensory awareness', solitude and silence in learning. These concepts are listed in column three of Table 0.2. This kind of higher-order thinking leads to further questioning, such as: 'Why are the senses so important for learning?' Both natural environmental and social phenomena affect the senses in a profound way. Natural light and dark, natural smells and taste, natural sights and sounds form a largely unappreciated backcloth to our everyday experiences. The social world, of people, buildings, machines, advertising and mobile phones continually bombards our senses with stimuli. It is interesting that when we go on holiday we are often filled with excitement, and this excitement is largely due to the sensitizing or awakening of our senses. We become exceptionally receptive to the experiences around us; our senses open up and become extra responsive to stimuli. We hear the voices as new and different, experience the bus or train as different, smell the air as different, and see the sky as different, even though it is the same sky as back home. At home and work these senses can be dulled – the same train or tram into work, the sky that is there each day yet we read the paper on the bus, the food that is the same, the language and voices that are the same. So it is with education and training. Long slide presentations can often typify the phenomena of sensory dulling.

So how do we open up the senses for learning? How might we push the sense 'refresh' button? Lectures and presentations can be more stimulating as a result of sensory engagement. In a typical lecture the senses most engaged are those of hearing. If a presenter holds up a fleece jacket made of recycled bottles, the sense used is that of seeing. If a carpet made out of corn is shown, the senses engaged are those of seeing. If these artefacts are then passed around so that people can feel them, then the experience of the softness of the plastic fleece and the hardness of the carpet engages the senses (see, for example, Chapter 3.1). The sensory engagement is stepped up beyond merely telling and explaining the phenomena, and it is multiplied, thus engaging, in sequence, more than one sense. Video clips are multi-media moving images engaging the senses, and they can be utilized, perhaps emerging out of a still photograph on screen to stimulate interest. Traditional presentations or lectures can be altered from a predominantly oratory experience to a multi-sensory experience potentially engaging and including a broader range of learner senses (Laird, 1985; Mayer, 1997) (see, for example, Chapter 5.5). There are potential problems associated with increased stimulation in, say, using technologies to support learning: one argument is that technology and the overuse of media can create sensory flooding or sensory overload. These are further conceptual areas open for investigation in practice. Few spaces exist today (low stimulation levels or silence) to enable people to think, empty out or rewire the brain. Silence is a sensory extreme. Silence and complete darkness are sensory experiences that are increasingly difficult to find, yet they can help to gain access to the inner self. Beyond the ephemeral nature of overstimulation lie reflective or meditative mind states that can present powerful experiences for learning: stillness and quietness can confer inner peace and calm. Thus, at the more complex level, the role of sensory intelligence in understanding our 'belonging' and 'being' (the first and last columns in Table 0.2) requires the experience of an advanced level of mind state, a consciousness referred to as 'no-mind' states that lie beyond material 'form', beyond mere 'activity'. These examples illustrate the existence of conceptual areas that require consideration and further investigation in practice.

Experiential learning: the fundamental theoretical positions

The question 'What is experiential learning?' is difficult to answer, partly because experiential learning has been subject to many interpretations, with many writers developing their own theories, models or concepts over the years. Few have been specifically aimed at helping educators and trainers develop an understanding of the art and science of experiential learning.

Experiential learning has been interpreted in many different ways in different parts of the world within many different professions. Whilst a plethora of writers has contributed to these deliberations, a common definition of experiential learning remains elusive: to some extent such a definition might even be impracticable.

A misinterpreted Eastern lineage?

Experiential learning has a long history, and of course the story of this evolution can be revealed in many different ways. The view presented here is that the practice of experiential learning is very diverse in its global form. It has suffered from some cultural misunderstanding and misinterpretation along the way. Let me give one example. Confucius's (551–479 BC) well-known aphorism 'I hear, I forget; I see, I remember; I do, I understand' laid the early foundations, the lineage, for subsequent Western interpretations concerning learning from experience. This simple summary transmits an important principle: it seems, in the West at least, that if we are simply told, then we forget; if we watch, we might remember; but if we do the real thing, this is the best way to learn. This quite clearly informed the 'Tell, show, do' instructional model developed by Edgar Dale (1969).

Aphorisms do not offer detail – such a Confucian saying is open to interpretation within the language of the 'Chinese way'. If it is translated at face value it can so easily lose its original Eastern meaning. 'Doing' is perhaps better inter-preted as 'practice': in this sense engaging the whole person. 'Learning by experiencing' was meant to be interpreted in its richest possible sense. Let me offer a slightly more exacting translation of the saying for you to ponder. I want you to at least imagine a Confucian philosopher saying it in a 'Chinese way':

To hear something is better than not to hear it,
To say something is better than just to hear it,
To know something is better than just to say it,
To practice something is better than just to know it.

To practice is to experience it, to feel it, to sense it, to understand it and to immerse yourself in its richness, by doing it regularly, for yourself.

The notion of a richer experience: the 'giraffe effect'

This rich notion of an immersion in an experience can be explained through a simple zoological metaphor (the author initially trained as a zoologist). Giraffes are usually seen in zoos, but some people may have been fortunate enough to see them roaming in the wild. In both these settings, however, this large and remarkable animal is observed from a distance, either in a cage or roaming around free. Recently safari parks have created a very different experience, one that allows people to stroke and feed a giraffe from a car. The experience of stroking the giraffe gives a very real impression of its enormity. The smell of musky urine in its body scent can be quite overpowering. The gaze of the large black eyes, the dripping saliva from the long, sandpaper-like tongue as the giraffe nuzzles through the car window to take food from one's hand is a much richer experience than the traditional distance view. This is perhaps what expe-riential learning should be like – the richness engages us, and the experience takes centre stage as core material for learning.

The learning shift is from distance to immersion, from transmission to transformation.

The experience has an outer-world dimension to it, as well as an inner-world dimension. The connectivity and interaction of the outer and inner world experiences are central to whole-person philosophies of learning. It is easier to observe, work with and 'read' the outer, more public world experience of the experience of engaging with a live giraffe. This outer 'being' is related to the where of learning, a belonging and connectedness to other people, and to place and space. The internalization of an experience into the inner world of the body, into a feeling dimension (hearts) and a cognitive dimension (minds) is less easy to read in others: this is a more private world.

Partly because of its long history, views about experiential learning do tend to differ widely. Outdoor adventure therapy specialists might see experiential learning in a very different light from corporate learning and development specialists or higher-education academics. Experiential learning does not have to involve people being physically active, and experiential learning about nature and the environment, outdoor learning, adventure learning and outdoor therapy, with a few notable exceptions, are typically left out of the work of the more distinguished contributors on the subject: this may simply be because they have not experienced this area at first hand and so feel unable to comment.

In 1989 experiential learning was said to comprise four main areas or villages: 1) the accreditation of prior learning; 2) the changing of formal education; 3) community action; and 4) personal growth and development (Weil and McGill, 1989). These villages have now evolved and diversified into many smaller hamlets: experiential learning is thus a diverse concept and one that is certainly not the exclusive domain of formal education or learning at work. Experiential learning is thus a constructed term that continues to evolve.

Definitions of experiential learning

Experiential learning is a term that has many ideologies and meanings and because of this it is problematic, particularly when attempting to establish defining boundaries. Some debates centre around the extent to which experiential learning might even embrace life itself (Fenwick, 2003: 87) because the concept has moved on to the point where the 'distinction between experience and non-experience becomes absurd' (Fenwick: ix). Trying to find an overarching concept or model is thus also fraught with problems, not least because models are always problematic because they can be seen as either too simple in their representation or too complex to commit to practice or to memory.

The Chinese aphorism and cyclical models such as that of David Kolb (1984) are relatively simple and memorable guiding principles, useful in the design of experiences for learning. The Chinese aphorism is best understood when the principle of learning by doing is interpreted as a whole-person philosophy, where the broad notion of 'doing' as experiencing something is a rich and sophisticated immersion, involving our inner and outer worlds in a connected way. A whole-person philosophy embraces thinking derived from different disciplines, including biology, neurophysiology, psychology, and social and environmental sciences. The whole-person definition offered here gives a broad definitional context for the purposes of this book, in an attempt to find a balanced, connective approach to learning and where the experience takes centre stage:

a sense-making process involving significant experiences that, to varying degrees, act as the source of learning. These experiences actively immerse and reflectively engage, and the inner world of the learner, as a whole person (including physically, bodily, intellectually, emotionally and spiritually) with their intricate 'outer world' of the learning environment (including being and doing – in places, spaces, within social, cultural, political context, etc) to create memorable, rich and effective experiences for and of learning.

This is of course a very broad and somewhat rudimentary definition. Edward Cell in his book, *Learning to Learn from Experience*, referred to a definition offered by Keeton and Tate back in 1978. Cell was highlighting the differences between academic learning and experiential learning, and the definition quoted referred to experiential learning as:

Learning in which the learner is directly in touch with the realities being studied. It is contrasted with learning in which the learner only reads about, hears about, talks about, or writes about these realities but never comes into contact with them as part of the learning process.

Keeton and Tate, 1978, cited in Cell, 1984: viii

Interestingly the Keeton and Tate text was titled 'Learning by Experience – what, why and how'. The immersion in, and contact with, the experience is thus perceived as very important. The experience takes centre stage: it is the foundation of, and the stimulus for, learning. This is the core argument in much theoretical work on experiential learning. That is why the core dimensions of the experience of learning form the focus of this book.

Experiential learning: assumptions and connotations

Several theories and associated modelling are more frequently drawn on by educators and trainers than others. Some of these models are simple, some more complex, some are more theoretically anchored, some more practically anchored. Many models are very basic triangular, circular or spiral sequential constructions. The famous triangular model known as the 'Tell, show, do' triangle was created by Edgar Dale (1969) and represents the concept of good instructional technique. It has clearly been founded on the Eastern aphorism mentioned earlier. Then there are the circular models of the learning cycle and the training cycle. These appear in many education and training texts to support the design processes, and these soon became referred to as the 'orthodoxy of the training profession' (Taylor, 1991: 258). The learning cycle of David Kolb (1984) is the most ubiquitous. It builds on the centrality of doing as the concrete experience. Kolb creates a four-stage model known as the learning cycle: the concrete experience, followed by reflection on the experience, followed by abstraction and application. This cognitively based model is variously described as aiding the design process (Brant, 1998), as 'part of the terrain of learning' (Usher and Edwards, 1994: 1992), 'the most widely adopted pedagogic method' (Rea, 2007: 122). It remains popular as an aid to both education and training partly because of the logical sequencing of the learning activities: it presents four simple stages to effective learning as a cyclical model. Here the usefulness for trainers and educators is that learners require time to reflect, to process their concrete experiences, think of new ideas and then apply them. This model is based on the notion of a 'construction' of learning, in the minds of the learner, and so it is regarded as a constructivist theory of experiential learning with a clear focus on the importance of reflecting on what has happened as a result of the concrete experience.

Some writers argue that this famous learning cycle, whilst extremely influential in management education in the United States and the UK, is rarely seen as problematic (Reynolds, 1997; Holman *et al*, 1997; Jarvis, 2004). These authors consider that the learning cycle overlooks and mechanically explains how learning works but seems to divorce people from the social, historical and cultural aspects of self, ie the focus is on the cognitive, internal learning processes of the 'brains' of the individual learner (Illeris, 2002). Many authors also maintain that the fieldwork and experiential thinking behind this circular model are lacking, in terms of the lack of fieldwork with different people from a range of cultures, gender, ages, socio-economic and educational backgrounds. From a learning and teaching perspective this cyclical model is regarded as simplistic, overly mechanistic and formulaic (Rowland, 2000; Moon, 2004) and limited in terms of its application to the design of teaching and learning.

The learning cycle and the training cycle when combined can create a figure of eight: they join at 'experience', a significant connectivity.

This linked model suggests that the differential between trainers and learners is reducing, as they jointly choreograph the dance of learning: as co-learners, with knowledge as co-constructed, and with learners educating and training others in order to learn from their teachings. What follows is that the classrooms will change, as form accommodates these new functions.

Experiential learning is based on a set of general assumptions about learning from experience. Table 0.3 compares the general assumptions developed by Boud, Cohen and Walker in 1993 with those outlined by Jenny Moon in 2004.

In this book, 'connotations' and 'assumptions' are explored in a practical sense. These include an exploration of construction, deconstruction of and reflection on an experience, the nature of experimentation and the holistic processes involved in learning, the role of emotions and the body and the social dynamic involved in learning.

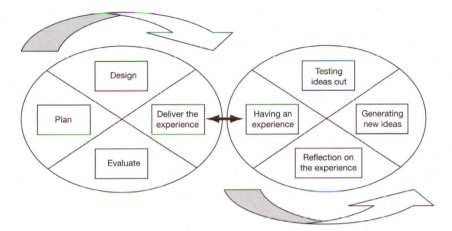

Figure 0.2   *Linking the training cycle with the learning cycle*

Table 0.3   *Assumptions and connotations in experiential learning*

Boud, Cohen and Walker (1993) developed core *'assumptions'* in experiential learning theory	Moon (2004) developed core *'connotations'* in experiential learning theory
Experience is the foundation of, and the stimulus for, learning	The material for learning is usually direct experience
Learners actively construct their own experience	It is not usually mediated or taught
Learning is a holistic process	There is often the sense that experiential learning is a favoured manner of learning, is better, more meaningful or empowering
Learning is socially and culturally constructed	There is usually reflection, either deliberately or non-deliberately, involved
Learning is influenced by the socio-emotional context in which it occurs	There is usually some active phase of the learning ('action', 'doing', 'experimentation' and so on)
	There is usually some mechanism of feedback present
	There is usually formal intention to learn

Constructivist theories or approaches to experiential learning have received critical commentary that questions the simplicity and degree to which the experience is constructed in the minds of the learner: all these critical positions collectively present a central consideration, a questioning, about the extent to which experiential learning is socially, psychologically, environmentally or otherwise constructed. Fenwick (2003) has produced an overview of some of these alternative views or theories of experiential learning that reinforces the centrality of this debate. Fenwick explores psychoanalytic theories, which focus on the inner-world unconscious desires of learners and how the unconscious impacts upon the conscious state. Critical cultural theories are then explored in terms of how experiential learning might relate to power, authority and culture in the outer world, and how attending to such issues might transform social order. Situative theory is then explored in terms of how it focuses on the immersive participation and learning within communities of practice. Finally, Fenwick explores ecological theory and experiential learning in terms of the complex relationships between cognition and the outer-world 'environment' in which learning occurs.

Experiential learning: adopting a balanced approach

A vast array of literature exists on experiential learning. A core notion is that experiential learning differs fundamentally from what Carl Rogers termed the 'Jug and mug approach' to learning or what Paulo Freire (1970) called the 'banking approach' to learning. Experiential learning is not didactic, passive or rote learning, where the learner is passive, absorbing the expertness of the given. Experiential learning tends to be more active than passive but not solely in the physical sense. Active engagement might take on dimensions of the physical, the sensorial, the emotional, the cognitive, the bodily, or the inner psyche; however, too much focus on one dimension can lead to an imbalance in the experience. Any emergent experience can present a learning opportunity; it can emerge spontaneously, right there in front of us, or it can be planned in a proactive way to richly engage us with the many dimensions of the experience. Any rich experiences can bring about significant change, and deep forms of change are referred to as transformational. A learning experience can be both positive and negative. Heron (2001), writing about 'whole person' approaches, believes that the perfect life web is never complete, but often torn and damaged in places. At times negative experiences are less likely to be seen as learning experiences, but with hindsight, and with careful reflective thought and processing, they can make us stronger. They are important to the sense of being and 'becoming' a person, of developing a sense of self.

Throughout this book many simple concepts are introduced. Simple models of learning usually take the form of waves, triangles or circles. In the course of life we experience 'waves' of high energy followed by calm, and these underpin our daily experiences. Life is certainly an emotional rollercoaster of ups and downs and this is typical of a 'rounded', 'balanced' life. Waves similarly influence the experience of learning. After expending much energy on learning activities, people might then find space and time to reflect and relax. But some waves of activity are shallow waves. There are also deeper ones, short ones and long ones, as in the ocean itself:

> The little waves we see lapping the shore are in fact carried on the waves that are nine ordinary waves long. These waves are themselves carried by waves that carry nine of them and these larger waves are similarly carried by waves that carry nine of them. Some waves in the ocean are miles long.
>
> Buzan, 2000: 200

A good learning experience involving a group of people would be inclusive, allowing a diverse range of people to engage, to 'catch a wave'. Each person has a different story of the experience, and a balanced approach to learning recognizes differences in people. The difference is acknowledged and positively worked with. These differences might be gender, culture or they might take the form of differences in literacy ability or preference (eg emotional literacy, visual literacy, sensory literacy, storied literacy and digital literacy). Many of the dualisms restrict our lives, and cause imbalance to learning. The oppositional states listed below underpin how we are and who we are in the world. Experiential-learning practice benefits from a 'balanced' consideration of these illustrative states:

- East–West;
- culture–nature;
- modern–primitive;
- material–spiritual;
- object–subject;
- natural–human;
- natural–artificial;
- outer–inner world;
- sense reception–perception;
- primary–secondary experience;
- mind–body;
- task–process;
- social–psychological;
- affect (emotion)–cognition (reason);
- conscious–subconscious;
- formal–informal;
- real–simulated;
- challenge–support;

- energy–tension;
- male–female;
- positive–negative experiences;
- play–work.

The layout of this book

This book is designed to celebrate the connectedness of practical experiential knowing with theoretical knowing. A rich understanding occurs when these two forms of knowing are linked. All the learning experiences described in this text fit the model in various ways: they all address an aspect of the chosen overarching six dimensions of learning, ie belonging, doing, sensing, feeling, knowing and being. Each of the six dimensions of learning is presented in a separate section of the book. Each section contains a descriptive overview of the theoretical concepts, followed by five detailed but illustrative learning experiences. Each dimension contains an overview with four simple headings:

1. A simple title.
2. A brief explanation of the main issues that require a degree of appreciation when attending to this dimension.
3. A brief explanation of a number of concepts that can be developed and worked on.
4. An overview of five activities that follow, so as to conceptually locate the experience within the overarching model.

The five experiences in each dimension contain the following headings:

- A popular and memorable title, almost as a brand name;
- A subtitle explaining the broad focus of the activity;
- What it achieves;
- Underlying principles;
- How to run it;
- Resources required;
- Tips;
- References and/or further reading.

A complete summary of all the experiences, showing both the practical and theoretical focus, is shown in Tables 0.4 to 0.9, which together represent the complete experiential framework.

Table 0.4   *Dimension 1 – belonging: five experiences focusing on the where*

Experience 1.1	Popular title: Just four steps
Linkages	Illustrative practical focus: customer service
	Conceptual focus: the creative use of space; learning linked to bodily movement, relating space and cognition
Experience 1.2	Popular title: Coffee and papers
Linkages	Illustrative practical focus: learning through relaxed reading (any subject) in individually selected spaces; followed by group stories of the interpretations of the readings, thus developing a 'collective' understanding and interpretation of a topic
	Conceptual focus: private individual space, associated with a solo mental state of relaxed alertness; a mood and ambience are created to enhance the experience; subsequently linked to collaborative social learning and the notion of a collective brain
Experience 1.3	Popular title: Edventure
Linkages	Illustrative practical focus: complex icebreaker; getting to know people, culture and selected, significant places
	Conceptual focus: immersive experiences, in new spaces and places, with new social, natural and cultural dynamics
Experience 1.4	Popular title: Different ways to know
Linkages	Illustrative practical focus: creative thinking
	Conceptual focus: information mobility and spatial relational thinking; people and active learning/movement; vertical and horizontal mapping
Experience 1.5	Popular title: Listening to silence
Linkages	Illustrative practical focus: focused sense of belonging in different spaces and contexts; four simple exercises using silence, rhythmical activity, meditation, focused sensory work to access the inner self
	Conceptual focus: meditative, 'no mind' states, used to develop presence and self-awareness

Table 0.5 *Dimension 2 – doing: five experiences focusing on the what*

Experience 2.1	Popular title: Bike it!
Linkages	Illustrative practical focus: analysis of individual and group dynamics: team building, leadership, communication, interpersonal work; can be adapted to develop financial skills in less-experienced people
	Conceptual focus: construction and deconstruction (of objects, artefacts, theories, etc) in problem-based learning (PBL)
Experience 2.2	Popular title: Altering reality
Linkages	Illustrative practical focus: negotiating skills development
	Conceptual focus: raising and/or lowering the degree of perceived realness within an experience of learning
Experience 2.3	Popular title: Read all about them
Linkages	Illustrative practical focus: getting to know people in a group (introductions) while learning to write introductions to business reports or assignments
	Conceptual focus: matching or analogous experiences
Experience 2.4	Popular title: Antiques Roadshow
Linkages	Illustrative practical focus: developing product expertise in employees; from mobile phones and technological equipment to hair and beauty products and practical outdoor tools and equipment
	Conceptual focus: using sensory awareness and a morphological approach to the reading of materials; leads to the development of new knowledge and understanding
Experience 2.5	Popular title: Hearing voices
Linkages	Illustrative practical focus: customer service; voice work: reception and call-centre training
	Conceptual focus: increasing or lowering complexity; sequence, shape and flow in learning experiences

Table 0.6   *Dimension 3 – sensing: five experiences exploring the how*

Experience 3.1	Popular title: Brand sense
Linkages	Illustrative practical focus: brand development and the role of the senses; the customer experience
	Conceptual focus: multiple sensory stimulation for learning, particularly for association and memory
Experience 3.2	Popular title: Blindfold
Linkages	Illustrative practical focus: communication
	Conceptual focus: sensory blanking, substitution and amplification
Experience 3.3	Popular title: Shape and colour
Linkages	Illustrative practical focus: unlocking self and group awareness: enabling the divulgence of personal information
	Conceptual focus: projection – onto objects; memory 'door handles'; learning preferences/styles
Experience 3.4	Popular title: The rucksack and the fleece
Linkages	Illustrative practical focus: sustainable product development, sustainable development awareness
	Conceptual focus: stepped sensory stimulation linked to intellectual engagement and curiosity; mediating artefacts and learning with large audiences
Experience 3.5	Popular title: Nuts and bolts
Linkages	Illustrative practical focus: the development of systematic skills associated with, for example, filing and storage systems, time management and the classification of objects from living species to nuts and bolts and screws and nails. The skills introduced here are those of sorting, classification, organization, justification and defence of chosen systems, and critical analysis
	Conceptual focus: somatosensory stimulation and visual acuity linked to higher-order cognition

Table 0.7   *Dimension 4 –* feeling*: five experiences exploring the emotional domain (heart)*

Experience 4.1	Popular title: Ace of spades
Linkages	Illustrative practical focus: reflection and reviewing
	Conceptual focus: accessing the feelings dimension, using popular objects that shift people through four stages of reflection/review; physical movement of groups of people into four separate spaces for collaborative discussion
Experience 4.2	Popular title: Accessing emotions
Linkages	Illustrative practical focus: generates group discussion of feelings dimension in learning experiences
	Conceptual focus: accessing emotions, using varied metaphors: visual, word, phrase and object metaphors
Experience 4.3	Popular title: Reframing, rewriting, rethinking
Linkages	Illustrative practical focus: dealing with fear and anxiety in learning, eg fear of presentations
	Conceptual focus: reframing inner voices, changing scripts to alter underlying emotions that create fear and anxiety
Experience 4.4	Popular title: Unfinished statements
Linkages	Illustrative practical focus: developing a reviewing booklet to explore a range of emotions and feelings experienced while learning
	Conceptual focus: affective prompting; pair work sharing emotions and feelings; altering prompting sequences
Experience 4.5	Popular title: String lines
Linkages	Illustrative practical focus: reviewing small and large learning journeys (eg organizational, educational, parenting, expeditions, retirement, life)
	Conceptual focus: exploring and sharing the typical emotional roller-coaster nature of life journeys

Table 0.8   *Dimension 5 – knowing: five experiences exploring cognition (mind)*

Experience 5.1	Popular title: The marketplace
Linkages	Illustrative practical focus: innovation and creativity, sustainable development, corporate social responsibility, product design
	Conceptual focus: the development of higher cognition: structure and pattern, relation, comparison, analysis, synthesis, convergence, divergence and deduction
Experience 5.2	Popular title: How to get to work...
Linkages	Illustrative practical focus: an exploration of how to get to higher understanding; forms of knowing (eg in MBA programmes, etc)
	Conceptual focus: oscillation between different forms of knowing; building on everyday knowing to develop abstract, propositional knowing from everyday experiences
Experience 5.3	Popular title: The Singapore obelisk
Linkages	Illustrative practical focus: problem solving, group dynamics and communication
	Conceptual focus: MI theory; mathematical-logical intelligence
Experience 5.4	Popular title: Skills for researching and consulting
Linkages	Illustrative practical focus: an experiential approach to practitioner–researcher training; the links and differences between consultancy and research
	Conceptual focus: developing complex skills using a stepped journey from cognitive simplicity to cognitive complexity; using popular metaphors to create an experiential approach to learning
Experience 5.5	Popular title: Walk the talk
Linkages	Illustrative practical focus: understanding complexity – systems or interrelated information – at work or in education (eg finance systems, the history of social or environmental movements, teaching philosophy, learning complex systems at work)
	Conceptual focus: linking kinaesthetic, spatial-relational awareness to mind, body and voice; collaborative learning; learners as researchers and producers of their own learning materials

Table 0.9 *Dimension 6 –* being: *five experiences exploring personal awareness and change*

Experience 6.1	Popular title: Cards on the table
Linkages	Illustrative practical focus: personality
	Conceptual focus: self-selection and choice in self-awareness
Experience 6.2	Popular title: Comic strips and newspapers
Linkages	Illustrative practical focus: reflection – story creation
	Conceptual focus: innovative visual-digital individual and group reflection and self-awareness
Experience 6.3	Popular title: Behavioural awareness
Linkages	Illustrative practical focus: social behaviours – interactions such as meetings/events
	Conceptual focus: behaviour analysis and self-sensitization
Experience 6.4	Popular title: Service learning
Linkages	Illustrative practical focus: team and organizational development
	Conceptual focus: learning through corporate and individual giving, not getting; real projects and their impact on learning and motivation; service to the community and/or the environment; social responsibility and company values
Experience 6.5	Popular title: Unmasking
Linkages	Illustrative practical focus: self-awareness, playfulness and the making of masks
	Conceptual focus: the hidden persona; subconscious

Advanced understanding of conceptual linking across dimensions

The six dimensions are overlapping and clearly linked. The separation presented here is purely to focus on a single dimension. However, concepts can be explored in relation to more than one dimension. This begins the deeper understanding of the complexity of the interrelatedness of whole-person approaches to experiential learning. The following examples briefly illustrate this interrelatedness: between mind, body and space. The 'where' in learning, the spaces and places, are inextricably linked to the sensory-bodily dimensions of awareness, and to the mental processing we undertake. The following short examples highlight these relationships:

● Creative design. Art students at a UK university use three stages of creativity, adapted from creativity strategies used by Walt Disney. These stages involve the dreamer, the critic and the realist. The students actually dream their ideas up in one place, but they enter another different place to allow the critical voice to come through. A third place is used to voice more realistic considerations of their initial creative work. By using different places for the three different cognitive (brain) processings, the inner voices are separated and so do not battle against each other for dominance. They are separated out and dealt with one at a time.

- Reviewing and reflecting. This is an adaptation of one of the hundred reviewing techniques described by Roger Greenaway on his well-known and excellent website, www.reviewing.co.uk. Four processing elements of reviewing, called the four Fs, occur in this approach in four different spaces. First the 'facts' are discussed in one space, then the 'feelings' in another space, then the 'findings' in a third space, and finally the solutions or 'futures' are discussed in a fourth space. The use of different spaces, such as the four corners of a room, again usefully separates cognitive processing. This activity is described in detail in Chapter 4.1.

- Reading and thinking. This experience initially involves an individual reading in a quiet and personal space. It is followed by a collective discussion of the readings in another space. The two spaces each create a very different ambience, and completely different mental processing skills are utilized. This activity is described in Chapter 1.2.

- Memory retrieval. During a review of a two-day training session attended by staff of the UK National Health Service, participants could not remember what they did at one specific time during the first afternoon of the course. One person eventually got up and said 'We did something here and I remember we sat in a circle.' The whole group almost simultaneously remembered the session details. Here going to the space and visualizing the group in a circle triggered the memories of the experience. Space, cognition, memory retrieval and bodily movement are all closely interrelated.

- Understanding complexity. Complex things can be more easily interpreted and understood by integrating bodily movement, spatial awareness of significant events in time and space, cognitive processing through talking and thinking, and sensory stimulation. This interrelatedness is described and highlighted in detail in Chapter 5.5.

All these examples illustrate interrelatedness. They each show, in different ways, how the spatial dimension has to be understood in relation to other dimensions. This is key to a deeper understanding of experiential learning.

Guidance for educators and trainers

A simple desktop model, to replicate the six dimensions, can be easily built using six polystyrene cups. They swivel nicely to show the principle of the model and each cup can have written on it the major themes or categories that need to be worked on.

This book focuses on linking a little of the theory with a lot of the practice of experiential approaches to learning. It offers many practical tools that address the main factors to consider when developing and delivering learning exercises for yourself, employees, youth groups, and, to a lesser extent, even schoolchildren. Most of the ideas can be translated into learning activities for anyone who wishes to learn more deeply and effectively.

The activities can be developed for distance-learning designs and virtual environments, and for typical classrooms, training rooms or other residential centres. I encourage you to develop exercises that make use of both the indoor and outdoor environments, whether at the top of a mountain, in a cave, on or under water or in an urban environment as was explored in *Experiential Learning: A Best Practice Handbook for Educators and Trainers* by Colin Beard and John P Wilson.

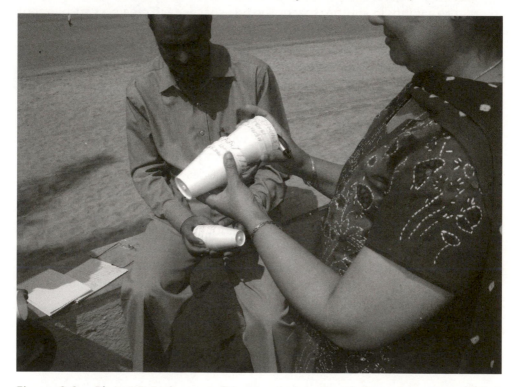

Figure 0.3   *Bharat Petroleum staff in Mumbai, India, working with the model of six dimensions*

Table 0.10 *A checklist for mediation and facilitation*

Focus on the *whole person and their experience* of learning, and keep this at the heart of all learning activities.
Be open to the constructs and beliefs of others; be open to alternative views.
Avoid manipulative approaches to learning as a form of human engineering.
Listen to learners and encourage all present to *take responsibility* for learning.
Engagement through mediation is useful but it is also sometimes good to leave learners hungry for more, and to steer people towards other forms of learning, eg self-directed.
Actively develop a collaborative climate that engages *everyone* (even though competitive strategies are employed at times!).
We learn by being *open to what the experience is telling us*; listen out for the feelings dimension, and work with those more difficult ideas articulated by learners...
Adopt a *co-construction* approach... really do believe that as educators and trainers we can influence the construction of learning in the minds of adult learners.
Teaching and learning are not separate processes when working with adult learners, and learning evaluation should be a mutual activity.
The experiences described in this book can in some cases also be added together to form a learning sequence, offering a stepped approach to learning.
Make it *real and relevant*... anchor the work in real-world experiences, including real-world learner experiences; allow these to intertwine into the session in order to re-examine past experiences and develop new ideas.
Experiences can occur in both *planned and unplanned* ways.
Offer experiential techniques that revisit past experiences and allow learners to view them in a new light: these methods we call retrospective learning. Moving from the past to the present, we consider methods to improve immediate learning, which we call concurrent learning.
Create possibilities for learning by encouraging imagination and the projection of ideas into the future; this is *prospective learning*.
Learners can play a significant role in deciding the place of learning, the pace of learning, the methods, the materials and the evaluation of learning.
Develop the concept of balance in attending to the whole experience...
Use the model as a guide – leave the cups on your desk to remind you to ask six key questions and to check how you have covered the six basic categories.
Learn to explore the main themes; this will take time – there are 15 million combinations... and there are no specific right answers... this is not a mechanical method!
Don't be afraid to create new combinations rather than follow a book or copy what you have seen others do – the person who risks is truly free...
Apply the concept of balance: inner world–outer world; objective–subjective; natural–human; male–female; material–spiritual; conscious–subconscious; mind–body; fast–slow; calm–energy; reason–emotion...
Consider especially the taxonomy of learning, the ABC: affect, cognition, behaviour (emotion, knowledge and skill).
Plan around experiential waves, large ones and small ones, and medium size waves.
Don't let your practice get stale or left behind... those who are in love with learning are in love with life. Keep up with the future and find time to read and develop an ability to think deeply and critically.
The model can be used as a diagnostic tool for designing experiential programmes with learners or solely by learners.

The possibilities for learning experiences are limitless, and in this sense this book is not, and certainly never set out to be, a complete work. It is designed to encourage the evolution of practice, to develop learning approaches that solve complex challenges in life, to make new additions to the vast range of concepts that underpin experiential learning. It is hoped that this book will provide a contribution to the wider project of sharing thoughts about the connectivity between the theory and practice of experiential learning.

 # References and further reading

Beard, C (2008) Experiential learning: the development of a pedagogic framework for effective practice, unpublished PhD thesis, Sheffield Hallam University

Beard, C and Wilson, J (2002) *The Power of Experiential Learning: A Handbook for Educators and Trainers*, Kogan Page, London

Beard, C and Wilson, J (2006) *Experiential Learning: A Best Practice Handbook for Educators and Trainers*, 2nd edn, Kogan Page, London

Boud, D, Cohen, R and Walker, D (1993) (eds) *Using Experience for Learning*, SRHE/Open University Press, Milton Keynes

Brant, L (1998) Not Maslow again!: a study of the theories and models that trainers choose as content on training courses, MEd dissertation, University of Sheffield

Buzan, T (2000) *The Speed Reading Book*, BBC Worldwide Ltd, London

Cell, E (1984) *Learning to Learn from Experience*, State University of New York Press, New York

Dale, E (1969) *Audiovisual Methods in Teaching*, Dryden Press, New York

Egan, G (2001) *The Skilled Helper: A Problem-Management and Opportunity-Development Approach to Helping*, Wadsworth Publishing

Fenwick, T J (2003) *Learning Through Experience: Troubling Orthodoxies and Intersecting Questions*, Krieger Publishing Company, Malabar, FL

Freire, P (1970) *Pedagogy of the Oppressed*, Seabury, New York

Heron (2001) *Helping the Client: A Creative Practical Guide*, Sage, London

Holman, D, Pavlica, K and Thorpe, R (1997) Rethinking Kolb's theory of experiential learning in management education, *Management Learning*, **28** (2), pp 135–148

Illeris, K (2002) *The Three Dimensions of Learning*, Krieger Publishing, Florida

Jarvis, P (2004) *Adult Education and Lifelong Learning: Theory and Practice*, 3rd edn, Routledge/Falmer, London

Keeton, M and Tate, P (1978) (eds) *Learning by Experience – what, why and how*, Jossey-Bass, San Francisco

Kolb, D A (1984) *Experiential Learning*, Prentice Hall, Englewood Cliffs, NJ

Laird, D (1985) *Approaches to Training and Development*, Addison-Wesley, Reading, MA

Mayer, J E (1997) Multi-media learning: are we asking the right questions?, *Educational Psychologist*, **32** (1), pp 1–19

Moon, J (2004) *A Handbook of Reflective and Experiential Learning: Theory and Practice*, Routledge/Falmer, London

Payne, P (2002) On the construction, deconstruction and reconstruction of experience in critical outdoor education, *Australian Journal of Outdoor Education*, **6** (2), pp 4–21

Rea, T (2007) 'It's not as if we've been teaching them...': reflective thinking in the outdoor classroom, *Journal of Adventure Education and Outdoor Learning*, **6** (2), pp 121–134

Reynolds, M (1997) Learning styles: a critique, *Management Learning*, **28** (2), pp 115–133

Rogers, C R (1969) *Freedom to Learn*, Charles E Merrill and Co Publishing, Columbus, OH

Rowland, S (2000) *The Enquiring University Teacher*, SRHE/Open University Press, Milton Keynes

Senge, P, Kleiner, A, Roberts, C, Ross, R and Smith, B (1994) *The Fifth Discipline Fieldbook; Strategies and Tools for Building a Learning Organization*, Doubleday, New York

Taylor, H (1991) The systematic training model: corn circles in search of a spaceship?, *Management Education and Development*, **22** (4), pp 258–278

Tolle, E (2005) *A New Earth: Awakening to Your Life's Purpose*, Plume Books, London

Usher, R and Edwards, R (1994) *Postmodernism and Education*, Routledge, London

Weil, S and McGill, I (eds) (1989) *Making Sense of Experiential Learning*, Open University Press and Society for Research in Higher Education, Buckingham

Young, M (2008) *Bringing Knowledge back in: from Social Constructivism to Social Reality in the Sociology of Education*, Routledge, London

Part 1

The first dimension: belonging

Introduction

Focus

- Understanding the practical issues of working with the learning environment
- The important practice question here is: Where and in what contexts is the learning taking place?

The learning environment is the whole 'outer world' experience, the surrounding experiential milieu outside our mind and body. It is the 'where' of learning. It is concerned with our 'being' in a situated sense, a belonging in the world related partly to place and space, context and location. This outer world of belonging thus has a placedness. The question of where is complex, embracing the physical, social, cultural and the natural. This outer situated world affects the learning experience: it is important to attend to the following core conceptual areas.

Spaces and places

The milieu of spaces and places in which we learn is an important conceptual area that has been neglected, partly due to the fact that we can take our surroundings for granted. People experience the world very differently: a person may be in the same place as another person but each will construct and reconstruct an experience of place very differently – we observe and sense different things, and our experience of the world is informed by past experiences and future possibilities. This 'outer world' dimension of the learning experience can include formal or informal places and spaces, virtual or real places, natural or artificially constructed places, and from classrooms out into urban and rural communities. The learning environment also affects mood and sets the ambience. The numerous places and spaces for learning are covered in more detail in *Experiential Learning: A Best Practice Handbook for Educators and Trainers* by Colin Beard and John P Wilson (Kogan Page, 2006). The coverage includes learning on land and water, in sheds and on ships, in school classrooms and artificial caves, on ski slopes, climbing walls and concrete white-water rafting courses: all offer potential as places to learn. This emerging pedagogy of space and place is worthy of more consideration by experiential providers. There are many dimensions to consider in working with aspects of this 'outer world' experience.

Learning is literally and metaphorically breaking out of the confines of the boundaries of the traditional indoor classroom, partly aided by technology. Old classrooms were never designed by educators, facilitators or trainers, so it is not surprising that we need to create and utilize more places to learn. This is why the consideration of spaces and places for learning experiences is a relatively unexplored subject in texts on learning published before the current millennium; but this is changing apace. The design of learning space is a subject that is gaining interest. A new pedagogy of space and place is emerging. The design of indoor learning environments is beginning to receive more attention. It is no longer acceptable to delegate the responsibility to architects or facilities specialists to design spaces and places for learning. Learning, after all, is not a subject they have been professionally trained in.

Space to liberate the mind

The book and the computer screen may in fact be limiting our understanding of the world. They present information in a very limited, linear, chunked way. Fragmented portions of information on a page have to be turned over to see the next chunk. We see information presented in this linear format and our brain can sometimes struggle to reorganize it. Spatial connectivity cannot be seen through words on a screen. The film *Minority Report* demonstrates a glimpse of a future not so far away when large glass screens will show digital information that can easily be enhanced and manipulated. This creates the next generation of learning tools: less focused on getting information and more concerned with working with the information so that it can be seen and manipulated in different ways. Working creatively with information is therefore an area that is covered through several experiences in this book. The human brain can scan a vast array of data from the internet and elsewhere. Brain capacity will develop in both education and training. Glass surfaces have a bright future. Glass will allow technology to be superimposed onto its surface, and the world wide web of information will open up upon giant surfaces where the page and screen do not limit brain functions and abilities. A touch on the glass will convert scribbles into text or change the surface so as to let natural light into the learning when required or to block it out again when it is not wanted. The secondary function is as a window, and other functions will be contained within the glass. Powerful natural light will shine through. Light, after all, is a natural energizer.

Creativity: linking the processing brain to physical space

Using different space for different thinking modes (cognition) so as to create differing perceptual positions is an interesting concept used by the Walt Disney organization in its strategy for creativity. This strategy was based on an observation that there were actually three different Walts: Walt Disney the dreamer, Walt Disney the realist and Walt Disney the fierce critic. To prevent these inner voices fighting with each other one approach is to develop separate physical locations or spaces for each voice to be heard separately: the dreaming space, the realist space and the critic space.

This same method using physical separation according to the mental processing required is used in the reviewing experience developed by Roger Greenaway with four ace playing cards from a card pack. This activity is described in the feeling dimension experience called 'Ace of spades'. The cards are located in four physically different spaces: diamonds for hard facts, hearts to represent emotions, spades to represent the processing that leads to digging deeper into the feelings, and finally clubs, the shape card with the three lumps in it, representing the three life choices of: 1) leave it alone and do nothing; 2) remove it, walk away from the problem, issue or event; and 3) change it or modify the situation.

Space associations: opening memory filing cabinets

Finally, an interesting memory recall situation occurred recently after a National Health Service event where experiential learning techniques were explored in order to improve health service training in a variety of areas. The fifteen or so trainer–facilitators returned from the first event after a month or so and when a recap was attempted one session could not be recaptured. Some people felt frustrated and said it was in the back of their mind, and they knew that it was useful. There was a block and then a silence. One person got up after a short while and said 'We did it here, and we sat in a ring.' Almost immediately everyone remembered the session. By revisiting the location of the experience, the memory released details of the experience. This illustrates how contextual memory (where) is linked to episodic memory (the ability to recall events).

The outdoors and beyond

Learning experiences can also be influenced by nature and environmental features: for example, involving the participants in a team orienteering or treasure-hunt exercise over windswept moorland in winter will produce a very different experience from one that involves people sitting indoors completing a questionnaire. Watching the sun setting while you sit on a warm beach, hearing the crunch of fresh snow in the morning, feeling the hot sand on your bare feet: these are all sensations of the natural world that have a profound impact on our sense of being.

Learning about the history of petrol manufacturing through a long bullet-point screen presentation in a hotel boardroom will be a very different experience from learning about petrol manufacturing by taking a tour of several industrial sites. Learning about organizational development by reading journal papers or book chapters while you sit by a log fire with coffee and croissants has the potential to develop knowledge through an intense pleasure of reading of the text, through deliberate quiet-time reading retreat-like experiences that can then be followed by a rich, collaborative exploration of the different pleasures, readings and interpretations of the texts by those participating.

The outdoors can add many more dimensions to the notion of spaces to learn or learning environments; these influence the learning experience. For example, the elements of air, wind, fire, earth and water – and silence – can all be incorporated within learning experiences and activities. These primal forces can also aid learners with their exploration of their inner self, to discover new things and create personal enlightenment. Darkness and silence are also experiences used in outdoor adventure learning but less commonly used within traditional indoor education, or in training and development programmes, yet such experiences can provide a reciprocity in the human–natural interactions. They can be very powerful and encourage deep learning. Educators and trainers adopt either empathetic or combative approaches to working with or against the forces of nature. Sitting watching a fire has an ability to create meditative, no-mind states. The mind experiences quietness, a silencing of its own voice or voices.

The social

A predominant view is that learning is socially constructed: while this is partly true, this view can devalue the contribution of the non-social and extra-discursive (beyond conversations) dynamics of everyday life. The non-social world is usually referred to as the 'material' or 'physical' world by social constructivists. Such terms are inappropriate: the world includes the living non-human world, an ancient part of our heritage that does impact upon and influence learning and experiences. In outdoor learning and nature therapy the non-social living world plays a very important part in experiential learning. Our experience of the human world is, however, largely socially constructed: thus, for this dimension, cultural and political awareness, ethical behaviour and moral values, collaboration and competitiveness, taking and giving in communities and in the wider society all play a part in the experience of learning.

Scope of Part 1

Five main activities are presented in Part 1. In order to gain a more complete understanding of the belonging dimension, all five illustrative experiences are briefly explained below.

✓ Experience 1.1: Just four steps

This is an experience of learning that illustratively focuses on customer service, exploring both verbal and written customer complaints. The main concept illustrated and explored through this experience is the use of space in a creative way to enhance learning from everyday experiences. The learning is walked, in a physical or kinaesthetic sense, so as to create a sequence of steps that give explanation to what has been 'abstracted' from the everyday experiences of the learners as customers in airports, supermarkets, bars and restaurants.

The experience deconstructs everyday experiences and initially reduces wide-ranging experiences, through group discussion, into a limited number of steps that explain the essential customer service sequences that are usually gone through in customer service recovery. These essential steps can then be walked and (collaboratively) talked through. The walking and talking of the experience allow the steps to be remembered more easily, to be embedded in the memory. A bodily or kinaesthetic imprinting takes place in the brain. The bodily movement involved in this experience of learning is referred to as kinaesthetic learning, and so the simultaneous body movement and articulation of customer service issues are enacted as a double sensory experience.

This experience, when used with the learning of complex procedures such as company invoicing or legal procedures, uses spatial awareness of key sequences to aid comprehension. This concept of spatial awareness can be applied in many other creative ways.

This experiential activity establishes the relationship between different forms of knowing. Learning from everyday experiences are developed into more abstract, higher forms of knowing, so that they can be 'seen' and known in a different way. What is experienced then is a shift from experiential/face-to-face knowledge and practical everyday knowledge in customer service experiences to propositional or conceptual knowledge about customer service issues. With staff experiences of customers increasing over time, the simple steps can be refurbished beyond their initial simplicity so that staff knowledge adds new experiential detail to the steps.

✓ Experience 1.2: Coffee and papers

This experience focuses on the concept of relaxation experiences that aid learning processes like reading. This experience explores the use of spaces and places that might create states of relaxed alertness. The conceptual link is to the 'belonging' dimension of the model and an additional illustrative focus is on the relationship between 'belonging' (in relaxed spaces) and 'doing' (reading complex material for learning). This is akin to a retreat style of experience. Quiet solo reading in comfortable personal and special spaces develops a relaxed mind state during high-level thinking through the reading of complex literature. Senior executives complain they no longer have time to read (and think) with any depth. They are often too busy 'doing', and so this experience has been successful with such people.

After the solo reading experience the focus shifts to a social construction of the learning. A dynamic is created whereby a 'collective brain' develops learning through the sharing of the totality of the individual experiences.

✓ Experience 1.3: Edventure

An 'edventure' is a combination of education and adventure. The experience explores a new place, such as a village, town or city. It is an experience that links to the model in that there is an appreciation of the outer-world impact on learning, and the focus is on the social, cultural and political dynamics. New people come together to explore new places, and to make sense of local history and culture. This experience immerses people in a rich situational backcloth for learning. Edventure can be used as an icebreaker with a difference, such as an initial experience for people attending a training programme. This activity looks at our outer belonging relationship with surrounding people, local history and culture, and their role in the sense of place.

✓ ## Experience 1.4: Different ways to know

This experience focuses on the ability to see and interpret information in many different ways. The experience focuses on a conceptual area concerned with the interrelationship of visual literacy, the use of space and the movement of information in ways that aid learning. The kinaesthetic bodily mobility of both information and people assists learning. The spatial-relational organization of information generates different ways of thinking, and the experience is suited to the development of innovative and critical thinking.

✓ ## Experience 1.5: Listening to silence

This experience involves mind states that are said to be in state of flow. It involves a person reading in isolation. This activity can be used in many different outdoor or indoor environments. Finding special quiet time for deep personal reflection in a special place is the conceptual area addressed in this experience. Quietness and solitude and at times meta-thinking (the ability to think about thinking and become aware about being aware) are involved in this experience. The focus is on cultivating a degree of inner presence, so as to work creatively with the interaction of the inner self with the reading material that is presented. This initial individual or solo experience is in stark contrast to learning by active doing. The 'solo' is traditionally an experience of 'being' in special spaces: something that is well known in the outward-bound movement, although this usually involves being in wilderness or remote natural surroundings.

A range of other concepts to work on in the belonging dimension

1. The spaces and people and places for learning are potentially limitless. Consider the full potential of providing a range of places for people to learn, such as indoor or outdoor, public or private spaces, quiet or interactive space, community-located places, or connected and networked e-spaces. In outdoor experiential learning, the mountains, the sea, caves, the town and shops and cafés all provide interesting opportunities for learning.
2. Different learning environments are, more or less, suited to different learning activities, and so the dimensions of belonging and doing are interwoven.

3. Learning environments can be specifically selected for specific learning, for example spaces or places for:
   - reflection or relaxation;
   - reading or writing;
   - brainstorming or energetic tasks;
   - social group working (round table) or quiet individual space (pod);
   - innovation and invention (shed?);
   - meditative mind states.

4. Location can activate the memory of an experience.

5. Give consideration to the socio-political climate and the cultural context: who manages or owns or controls the spaces for learning?

6. Consider the ability of learners to manage their own spaces – flexibility and mobility (move-ability and removability) of the furniture and artefacts in a range of spaces can facilitate learning.

7. Consider the mobility and flexibility of information within virtual and real space – seeing information from different directions and moving information around in different ways in space are the key to creative thinking and alternative 'views'.

8. The sizes of book pages and computer screens limit our brain capacity in terms of seeing information or patterns. Large screens or large spaces allow the movement and reconfiguration of information or products, text or images. This will enable learners to see information differently.

9. Colour, smell and lighting influence moods and therefore learning.

10. Consider the variety of e2 learning environments (e2 = experiential electronic) and 3D immersive environments.

11. Learners might experience working with:
    - mobile learning (laptops);
    - social interactive learning (social media or web 2.0 technologies for networking learning such as MySpace, YouTube, Bebo, Second Life, etc);
    - connected learning (wireless/wired);
    - visual interactive learning (eg video conferencing);
    - audio interactive learning (eg audio files, teleconferencing);
    - augmented reality (eg implanted chips that enable people to feel each others' emotions, enhanced beyond the real thing, such as brain-scan data that has been augmented or enhanced for medical learning, flight simulators);
    - ubiquitous or 'everyware' learning software (almost imperceptible but everywhere around us… embedded in objects, surfaces, clothing or the body. Examples include using smart-clothing technologies or wearable computing, smart furniture, smart doors, floors and corridors within buildings).

Just four steps: customer service and customer complaints

What it achieves

This experience of learning assists learners to deal with both verbal and written customer complaints. This session uses the body for improved learning of the major sequences that arise when dealing with issues of customer service. Spatial awareness and bodily (kinaesthetic) imprinting are used in a creative way. Simple experiential techniques support learners in their understanding of the relationship between everyday experiences and three other forms of knowing derived from the experience (propositional/theorizing, experiential/face-to-face immersion, and practical knowing/skill).

Underlying principles

This activity helps learners voice their own experiences of customer service so as to be better able to recognize and value their experiential knowing at work. The diverse experiences that learners bring to the activity are important. The activity promotes learner theorizing about professional 'situations' through social interaction. Their own experiences are crucial to personal and organizational development. Ultimately the habit of learning from everyday-life experiences can develop more sustainable lifelong approaches to 'learning to learn'.

The session allows learners to collaboratively construct the common steps or stages that occur in a typical customer service recovery situation. The activity generates propositional knowing or elementary theorizing that is suited to the organizational context. The resulting outcome is often a unique interpretation of the theories that are found in textbooks on customer service.

The floor or a large table is used to create space for the creation of four or five critical steps that become the model of customer issues. Using kinaesthetic reinforcement the steps are walked and talked through. The mind and body remember the steps as a sequence of events. This session uses real scenarios to make the model come alive.

How to run it

Learners are asked to share their own stories of customer service experiences. These can relate to their experiences in bars, doctor or dentist surgeries, in airports, or in hotel check-in situations, for example. Each group is given the opportunity to summarize succinctly the findings of their group.

Figure 1.1.1   *Experientially created financial models being constructed on walls and floors in Taiwan. Courtesy Training Department, Nan Shan Life Insurance, Taiwan*

A story of a poor customer service experience (see below for a good example of a real story) is then told to a number of groups (three or four learners at each table) and they all are asked to say what they would do if they were responsible for the customer service complaints.

Each group then has to establish their common thoughts about the essential ingredients or steps that might occur in such a situation, focusing on what would need to happen to ensure customer service recovery. Participants discuss and pool their knowledge about a possible response as if they were to be handling the situation as professional staff working for the organization concerned. People often relate to the need to listen with empathy, and to find solutions, finally checking that the outcome is satis- factory with the customer. Solutions generate much discussion, with less- experienced people tending to offer upgrades to first class for everyone in the example outlined below!

The next stage involves looking at the similarities and differences between all the group ideas so as to offer up and build on a shared understanding of the possible outcomes. These are then discussed at length.

Five masking-tape squares are created on the floor (see photo in Figure 1.1.1) to represent the possible sequential journey (in time) of the customer service recovery responses forged by each group. Each group is given a set of five large cards to write on. Using two to three words only, no more than five common sequences or steps are identified and placed in the appropriate masking-tape square. If the participant cards are all very different, this is fine. However, there are usually some striking similarities.

An additional option is to ask half the group to explore the response from the customer perspective and compare and contrast the results with the organizational perspective.

Lay out a masking tape grid on the floor as follows with a maximum of five steps.

Step One	Step Two	Step Three	Step Four	Step Five
Two or three key words only	Two or three key words only	Two or three key words only	Two or three key words only	Two or three key words only

The essential steps are identified by each group and then walked as they talk it through with the other participants.

True story: in-flight complaint

The business-class flight from Manchester to Mumbai cost £1,800. When food was being served, the trolley arrived with me last of all. I looked through the rather glamorous menu, a brochure in fact detailing the experience of their chef, and at the back a whole page was devoted to the wine taster. On asking for my selected choice I was told there was none of that option left. The only option left was fish for the starter. I decided not to make a fuss and had fish.

When the trolley arrived for the main course, the stewards followed the same route and arrived again at my seat as the last business-class customers to be served.

I asked for my preferred choice and was told there was none left. The only option left was fish. When I said that I had fish for the starter, even though it was not my preferred choice, the staff simply repeated that the only choice available was the fish. 'I don't really want a main course of fish,' I said.

The staff could see that I was not happy with this business-class experience. I think it might be fair to say I had 'unhappy customer' written across my forehead. I declined the sweet course.

Eventually the chief steward came to my seat and crouched down beside me and said, 'I understand that you're not happy with the service, Mr Beard.'

Under these circumstances, what would the steward say and do?

Now the group is asked to deal with this situation by working through what each party might say and how the situation might end.

The steps can then be opened back out after the reduction process by furnishing each step with additional information derived from the experiential descriptions, such as:

1.   The first stage often is associated with dealing with the 'feelings' and might involve saying, in support of them, 'Yes, I see why... I can understand that you felt...' This stage involves active listening, understanding, paraphrasing and other empathic responses. In the feelings stage the facts are often hard to establish if people are upset or angry.

2. Eventually the 'facts' do need to be established and ascertained from the customers themselves. Hearing the customer voice as an explanation is important. The customer wants and needs to be heard.

3. In agreeing to find a 'solution' the word 'appropriate' is often added by experienced people, indicating that it wasn't appropriate to upgrade all such complaints to first class!

This learning experience, involving reduction and expansion of collaborative everyday knowledge, can help learners to acknowledge and develop their own professional expertise. It can be used to handle both verbal and written complaints.

Their responses can be compared with textbook theories (see below), and discussion can usefully explore the professional skills that could be taken from the session.

Question to the learners: What would you do as a customer in this situation?

Real images, real, recent and relevant stories and the real menu?

*Please note that this **real** customer service issue was resolved very professionally by the chief stewardess working for Lufthansa.

Figure 1.1.2   *Adding a further sense of reality?*

Each step can take some time to establish detail, before the group moves on. Sometimes, of course, the process gets stuck at one stage, and groups might discuss typical situations where this can happen – for example, when a customer is so angry that the process does not proceed to discussions about how a solution can be found.

These steps can be reinforced with mini role plays first by the trainer, for example in a hotel-room complaint, exploring how it might be dealt with both by a hotel manager and by a complainant.

It can be pointed out that the steps or principles are similar to the steps to assertiveness. It is said that there are a number of simple steps to assertiveness. These steps can be practised and honed so that they eventually become part of everyday life skills and professional practice. These skills can help with customer service issues, with negotiating, and can support productive personal relationships. Over time these skills can be further developed to include feelings assertion, saying 'no' and other assertiveness techniques.

The three essential steps are as follows:

Step one: actively listen to what is being said and then show the person that you both hear and understand them (other views).

Step two: say what you think or what you feel (your views).

Step three: say what you want to happen (change- or solution-centred language).

The customer response to the in-flight experience might be similar:

- State the facts – say what has happened.
- Listen to the response from staff and show that you have listened to the person, that you have both heard them and understood them.
- Say what you think or feel.
- Say what you want to happen – move towards a desired solution.
- Closure – offer some acknowledgement of a satisfactory or unsatisfactory outcome.

As experience develops within a group, the stages can become more complex. The four steps are like the London Underground map – they initially represent a simple map to help people get from A to B. However, the four or five steps can become insufficient as experience develops, and so creating more complex experiential modelling is essential. More complex modelling might build in or incorporate the following developed from more experienced customer service managers:

- Solutions need to be appropriate.
- Expensive gifts or generous offers might prove to be too generous and might not be what the customer requires!

- Some customers just cannot or will not be satisfied! How do you deal with these situations?
- People often just want to be listened to and made to feel special or important.
- Complaints require company logging and follow-up in order for the organization to learn from customer experiences.

The exercise can be adapted to deal with written complaints. A folder of letters derived from company complaints is presented to the groups. These are real letters giving and receiving complaints.

More general letters might be brought in by the group and can include asking to be let off a parking fine and the response, companies giving vouchers in compensation for poor service, letters that clearly do nothing except half-heartedly apologize, a threatening letter from a solicitor saying you have not paid their bill yet and suggesting they will take you to court and that your credit rating will be permanently affected, and so forth.

The groups are asked to look at the letters and judge them. They are also asked to examine the common format for effective complaining format and the most effective format for the response format.

The letters are analysed and the common sequence or steps involved in writing letters can be explored. Good-practice sequences can be related to other groups.

 ## Resources required

- Masking tape.
- Large cards to write on.
- Large stick-it labels.
- Real examples of organizational letters of complaint and associated company responses.

Tips

The following notes on assertiveness might help with skills development.

Assertiveness became part of many counselling courses in the UK during the early 1970s (for example, counselling courses at Keele University in Staffordshire). First in the United States and then the UK, within a new climate of freedom and equality it was recognized that people who previously had limited chances in life now had an opportunity to lead a very different way of life. What was missing, however, were the skill and ability of everyday working folk to speak up and take advantage of new rights without damaging the rights of other people.

This awareness of the rights of people and the sense of personal responsibility was the central goal of assertiveness, as was being confident, being able to say what it is that people wanted, to be honest with themselves and with other people.

Thomas Harris encapsulated the behavioural theories of transactional analysis when he created a simple model called 'The OK Corral', which sums up our feelings about ourselves and other people.

Table 1.1.1   *The OK Corral*

I'm OK You're not OK **Aggressive**	I'm OK You're OK **Assertive**
You're not OK I'm not OK **Depressive**	You're OK I'm not OK **Submissive**

It is said that there are a number of simple steps to assertiveness. These steps can be practised, and honed so that they eventually become part of everyday life skills and professional practice. These skills can help with customer service issues, with negotiating, and can support productive personal relationships.

The three essential steps are as follows:

Step one: actively listen to what is being said and then show the person that you both hear and understand them (other views).
Step two: say what you think or what you feel (your views).
Step three: say what you want to happen... (change or solution centred language).

 **Further reading**

An excellent source of information for further development of these skills is *Assertiveness at Work* by Ken and Kate Black, published by McGraw-Hill. Another excellent and well-known source of information is *I'm OK, You're OK* by Thomas Harris, published by Pan Books.

Coffee and papers: positive mood and reading retreats for learning

What it achieves

Coffee and papers generates high levels of learner engagement and knowledge generation through the process of a reading retreat. However, the experience is designed to generate a mind state of relaxed alertness along with personal comfort: the individual experience has to be in a place or space that learners find particularly relaxing and comfortable. The quiet solo experience is then followed by a collaborative group exploration and critical reading of the papers and articles that have been read, so as to work with the acquired group collective knowledge.

Underlying principles

This session uses space in a creative way and so the experience has been selected to illustrate how the environment, the place or space, plays an important role in learning. Individual and collective group spaces have to be differentiated. An additional principle is that the generation of a positive mood, a state of relaxation, can give pleasurable 'flow' experiences during the act of in-depth reading (of articles, papers, chapters or newspapers, etc). This is known as relaxed alertness.

Learners are offered a large choice of 'papers' to be read. The selection and deselection of reading material, ie the use of choice, is an important principle here. Ideally the material will cover a substantial area that is worthy of discussion.

Space creates the positive mood, as does the metaphor setting of the title of 'coffee and papers', taken from the idea of relaxing over a weekend while reading the newspapers. This session adopts an approach of a personal retreat (in spaces) if framed correctly. Relaxed alertness is critical. The experience has been tried with several thousand people around the globe. The session can:

● Improve levels of collaborative discussion in a course, develop critical reading and debate, introducing a literature base to a topic/subject.

● Use space and place in a creative way to develop the pleasure of informed discussion derived from reading of the text. Different spaces can be encouraged and tried out.

● Generate deeper thinking for managers that rarely have time to read (as well as being used for education, where students are said not to read enough). Higher cognitive processing skills are developed within a short space of time because of group collaborative sharing when the knowledge base is high from reading.

● Create a situation where participants sell the benefits of reading a particular text. Often people will ask if the articles can be copied and distributed. My response often is to encourage people to take on board that responsibility themselves and to use the opportunity to network and send each other papers.

Figure 1.2.3a   *Personal space (Regency-Hyatt grounds, Mumbai)*

Figure 1.2.3b   *Experiencing relaxed alertness during coffee and papers (Shenzen, China)*

How to run it

Set out all the papers on a table as if it was a library or newsagent shop. The papers should ideally all be focused on a specific reading theme, creating lots of choice. It may be preferable to add some difficult articles and some easy ones if it is felt some people might either find the material too difficult or that they possibly will respond to a challenge of more depth to reading.

The technique can work at many levels. Newspaper articles or short book chapters can be used for less advanced reading groups. However, newspapers can also be used for other purposes such as the scanning of different perspectives from a particular story. For more advanced groups such as senior managers, executives or postgraduate or doctoral students, slightly more complex articles and papers can be used.

Set the mood with care so as to generate the spirit of a personal reading retreat session, using the metaphor of lounging at home reading the Sunday papers. Ask participants to find an area of personal space, preferably away from all others, and to make sure that they feel very comfortable before they start to read. Suitable light refreshments can add to relaxation and enhance the experience.

Learners need to select a quiet calm environment with as few distractions as possible, and where it is comfortable. Corporate managers and executives have tended to use the many hotel spaces and grounds in a creative way. On one occasion coffee and croissants, and fruit and strawberries dipped in chocolate and log fires were available! Outdoor spaces are popular in warmer times. For senior managers and executives where learning and development take place in hotels, the session has mostly started at approximately 11.00 am, which would traditionally be a coffee break session.

Cafés have been used for this experience. Students have experienced this type of reading activity whilst getting their own breakfast and coffee shortly after the start of an early 9.00 am university lecture. Students can be told beforehand that this is going to happen at a particular time or it can be done as a semi-spontaneous surprise.

Allow between 30 and 60 minutes of quiet solo reading, depending on circumstances. The group then reconvenes and discusses first the technique and space issues, and then the feelings and mood created, ie the reading process. The group then discusses the content of the articles: what they liked and disliked, the strengths and weaknesses of the paper, and things that they might adopt or take away as useful for work or practice. This experience can result in some people 'selling the benefits' of a particular article, leading to people requesting all the copies. This can form the beginnings of a network where learners copy and send round material to each other.

 Resources required

- A large selection of articles (sometimes these can be reusable to save preparation next time).
- A variety of levels of article can be used.
- In the case of students, they are encouraged to read quality journal articles.
- Sufficient spaces for individuals to relax and unwind.
- Coffees and teas and biscuits and other refreshments as appropriate.

Tips

The exercise below for relaxation and meditative mood setting can be used beforehand or by individuals when they have found their spaces.

Fewer than 10 per cent of learners have reported an inability to have a positive experience of reading using this technique. Their difficulty is often associated with a lack of concentration at certain times of the day or an inability to understand/access a more difficult article.

The importance of reading for one well-known CEO of a global company (Interface Carpets), namely Ray Anderson, is highlighted by the fact that when he realized he had little understanding of the notion of sustainable development he started reading more widely and more critically about society and his role in it as a business leader. Reading changed his views, his business and his life. The company has gone on to be widely recognized as leading the way for sustainability in business and winning many awards for successes. The company has for some years shifted the focus from selling carpets that are simply disposed of by customers to that of providing a service. The company specializes in carpet tiles, which reduce waste. They also make carpets out of corn and other biodegradable materials. More information can be gleaned from their website. Significantly the dawning experience for Anderson, often referred to as an epiphany, was initiated through reading with an open yet critical mind.

The following are extracts from field notes from Coffee and papers sessions created by the author.

- Participants often take their shoes off, sitting or lying on comfortable sofas, with soft music playing. Coffee percolators bubble away, Earl Grey tea is on offer and lemon scents the air. The articles are from *People Management* and *Management Learning, Management Education and Development, People and Organisations, Training and Development, Industrial and Commercial Training, Sloan Management Review, Harvard Business Review* and many others. Hardly Sunday-morning reading!
- On another session one corporate executive, sitting with stockinged feet placed on a stool, sipping fresh coffee and eating croissants by a log fire, said: 'I am in heaven. I realize now how I am losing the power to read and think at a deeper level… I take things home at weekends with the intention of reading things but never do…'
- In one session a postgraduate student said: 'During these sessions, differing views concerning the same articles were discussed and new insights developed based on individual experience outside the articles. This led to a spin of ideas that spurred more new ideas, and reshaped some of my initial thoughts of the article.'
- In another session it was later reported that the reading experience in Coffee and papers had a profound effect on one or two people. They work for the NHS, where staff are rightly encouraged to use evidence-based practice. This ideally would involve time to read about clinical practice.

This, however, was not happening for a number of reasons including that of guilt when reading at work. The staff put forward what turned out eventually to be a successful proposal brought to senior managers under the umbrella of a primary care trust (PCT) 'Inspiration Award' scheme in 2009. The proposal included some of the following required actions suggested in order to implement this idea.

– Encourage staff to write reading time into their objectives.
– Develop a marketing campaign across the PCT showing that it is okay to sit and read clinical material.
– Provide education for managers to help them understand how to enable staff to absorb current evidence.
– Understand the cost of allowing staff time to absorb evidence, but also calculate and understand the cost, service and other benefits.
– Resources could also be purchased that could make reading easier.

The following extract from *The Creative Teaching and Learning Toolkit* by Brin Best and Will Thomas highlights how this idea has been carried out within whole schools:

The start to a school day can be very rushed, with assemblies, registers, and the giving out of notices and information. A more relaxed start can provide a pleasant change and lower stress levels. A number of schools operate a system whereby on one or more mornings a week the whole school falls silent and everyone reads – in some schools this even includes the school office and phones are taken off the hook! Reading material is available for anyone who forgets and comics, newspapers and books of all kinds can be read. The usual announcements are pinned up or displayed on screens instead of read out. These initiatives have helped to develop a sense of calm during what can be a very hectic start to the day, and have enabled students to enter a more appropriate state for learning.

Best and Thomas, 2007: 93

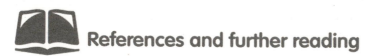 ## References and further reading

Barthes, R (1975) *The Pleasure of the Text*, trans R Miller, Cape, London
Best, B and Thomas, W (2007) *The Creative Teaching and Learning Toolkit*, Continuum International Publishing, London

Edventure: learning encounters with people and place

What it achieves

The activity opens up thinking about spaces for experiential learning beyond the hotel, boardroom or classroom. This experience involves learning about people and culture through connections with the external environment. Ideas are presented at both the local level and the international level.

Underlying principles

The experience aligns with the spirit of whole-person learning. Place and space, journeying, adventure and education are all linked together in these experiences, as important ingredients for learning – hence the title 'edventure'.

'Adventure' embraces many facets of people's lives and forms the basis of the experiential milieu. The dictionary suggests that adventure is a 'remarkable incident', 'an enterprise or commercial speculation', 'an exciting experience' or 'the spirit of enterprise'; and an adventurer is 'one who engages in hazardous enterprise'. To be an adventure an experience must have an element of uncertainty about it. Ideally and to varying degrees the outcome should be unknown, and the place or space should be unfamiliar.

The 'venture' part of adventure implies the element of travel, with or without a purpose. The many dictionary definitions of the term 'expedition' include that of a journey with a definite purpose. In expeditions there is also a target or goal, and a time constraint. An experiential learning 'journey' can thus be short, as in orienteering, or it can be longer and include major expeditions; or it can refer to a life journey. 'Outward bound' is a nautical term referring to the outward journey of a ship and the original outward bound schools had a strong focus on sea expeditions. Underpinning all of the ideas here is the key principle that the learner is on a journey. The physical journey or activity is an isomorphic representation of a wider learning journey. The physical journey can be orienteering, a short walk in hotel grounds or a distance travelled in kayaks. Physical activity is common on these learning journeys, used to manage the daily energy–tension balance, as physical exercise is known to be one of the most powerful positive regulators of mood, a subject examined in Chapters 5 and 6 in Beard & Wilson (2006).

Adventure, whether indoor or outdoor, requires an element of real or perceived risk to which the participant is exposed through engagement in an activity. This risk can be physical, emotional, intellectual or material.

A plethora of activities is currently on offer in locations around the world, offering adventurous travel as experiential education. Eco-adventure travel is an area that has increased rapidly over the last decade to become one of the leading areas of income for the tourism industry today.

How to run it

For this activity it might be more appropriate to ask who might help to run this activity for you. Many organizations offer such adventures. They often operate as voluntary charities delivering, for example, tall-ship adventures, gap-year adventures and similar activities. Examples are given at the end of this activity section.

Planning the journey, experiencing it and the learning from it are the key skills involved. The place of the journey is of enormous significance to the learning.

Local: just going into town

First a local experience is described. This can be variously used where a group of learners arrive in a new place, and have to work together for the first time. A journey into the town or city can be the site for the edventure. Such an experience can develop an unexpected deep sense of togetherness for a group of learners. It can even be used as a new form of experiential icebreaker.

It is important that learners are open to the spirit of this learning adventure and this new form of learning. A questionnaire can be used to raise awareness of the preparedness for new learning (see 'Planned and emergent learning: a framework and a method' by David Megginson, 1994, published in *Executive Development*). Megginson identified four different types of learners:

- Sleepers: who show little initiative or response to their experiences.
- Warriors: who plan their experiences but tend not to focus on learning from them.
- Adventurers: who respond and learn from opportunities that arise but tend not to create new opportunities for themselves.
- Sages: who both plan and learn from their experiences.

People can be dropped off at a specific location to work together in small teams solving a variety of problems, answering basic questions and probing into history, architecture, street names, statues and other cultural, social and natural phenomena. They also might be asked to carry out adventurous tasks such as busking in the streets. The journey might end with a group using consensus to identify a place where they would all like to eat. Eating together in small groups in different places is a fitting end to an evening of edventure. This kind of experience is informal and allows people to connect with a sense of locatedness in the village, town or city where they have come to learn.

Some more radical suggestions for alternative specific experiences that make deeper contact with the outdoor spaces and places are as follows:

- being inactive and alone in the town, quietening down, going inwards, inviting new thoughts in;
- sitting silently observing with someone else, sharing different perceptions of the town or village or city, focusing on natural things, walking differently from how one would in the city, slowly, silently, even blindfolded – and be open to some unfamiliarity;
- sitting or walking barefoot in natural places, making contact with soil or stone or grasses or water;
- focusing where possible on a meditative situation with another person, eg around a fire, seeing natural processes, life, the universe;
- telling, inventing and listening to stories;
- sleeping or lying for some time at night in natural spaces on the ground in a bivvy bag, expanding awareness, and dreaming.

International activities

Greenforce, Frontier and Earthwatch are three organizations that offer an unusual and new combination of learning journeys that we have termed edventure. These organizations construct a new form of multi-learning experience for people, containing a subtle mix of educative features for self-development: adventure, travel, environmental or community-development work and skills in scientific wildlife monitoring. These organizations are usually charities recruiting paying volunteers to support wildlife projects around the world.

Coral Cay is a not-for-profit organization at the cutting edge of eco-tourism that recruits volunteers to gather information about some of the world's most endangered coral reefs and rainforests around the world. Volunteers are trained in a range of skills including scuba diving, coral-fish identification and survey techniques. What is particularly interesting is that research shows that it is the 'learning' element that is the key motivational driver for those joining the organization as volunteers. Some of these experiential projects remain almost exclusively for those who have, or are able to raise, the necessary funds.

Greenforce was inspired by the commitments made at the Earth Summit in Rio in 1992 to identify and protect the biodiversity of the planet. One brochure is titled 'Work on the wild side! Conservation expeditions'. Volunteers are offered an 'experience of a lifetime'. These and many other practical environmental organizations grew out of the great demand for an educational 'experience'. Frontier is a non-profit organization promoted by the Society for Environmental Exploration, and has the following in its 2000 brochure:

> Taking part in a Frontier expedition is a once-in-a-lifetime experience... Future employers will be impressed with your achievements both in getting there and in succeeding in your project. Many former volunteers have used their expeditions as the basis for project and dissertation work for Bachelor's degrees and Master's degrees. Frontier is also a 'Sponsoring Establishment' for research degrees through the Open University, the *only* volunteer conservation organization to have achieved the status of a field university. If you want a career in conservation and overseas development work, Frontier is the only option. With all volunteers eligible for a level-3 BTEC qualification in Tropical Habitat Conservation just on the strength of 10 weeks of training and work on a Frontier expedition, becoming a volunteer gives you a chance to kick-start a career in this highly competitive field. A recent survey found that 62 per cent of ex-Frontier volunteers have achieved such careers thanks to their experience with Frontier.

Operation Raleigh selects young people to take on major expeditions around the world, and they too offer such projects in the international dimension of their development programmes:

> Challenges in the outdoors, and involvement in community or environmental projects, are well established as a successful means of developing

staff. Combining these with intensive international work in remote areas, Raleigh creates a framework within which learning can be transferred to the workplace. Working and living with people from different backgrounds for an extended period helps equip employees for today's fast-changing and demanding business environment. Working in real time, generating solutions to real problems, the experience proves sustainable and effective at developing the following qualities: team working, leadership, interpersonal skills, confidence, motivation and assertiveness, initiative, flexibility and resilience, adaptability, maturity, awareness of self and others.

Organizing expeditions to other places

Wilderness programmes exist in the United States and Australia that use expeditions that last over 100 days, and these are often used as times to reappraise life. They often result in powerful life-impacting learning and, as such, expeditions are still used by many organizations to offer development opportunities for young people in growth, self-development and active citizenship.

Adventurous journeys are used for youth- and adult-development programmes. In 1978 Operation Drake was launched in the UK. With its success, Operation Raleigh followed in 1984. Its aim was to develop leadership potential in young people through their experience of the expeditions. Operation Raleigh, renamed Raleigh International, sends 'venturers' between the ages of 17 and 25 years on a 10-week expedition. Expeditions are being increasingly used in many other ways, from management development to adventure tourism. The UK Institute of Management suggests that:

> There is growing evidence that expeditions are gaining an emerging prominence and profile within the realms of human resource development (HRD). Arising from this evidence is the acknowledgement that expeditions contribute to personal growth or development of desirable capabilities that are relevant to work contexts.

Advertising for such expedition packages is also increasingly found in management journals, and more adults are engaging in such life-enhancing journeys; even virtual expeditions can now be found on websites.

Among the personal growth themes emerging from research on expeditions are:

- increased tolerance and patience;
- increased awareness and appreciation of more basic things in life;

- a change in environmental values, eg recognizing how people use their cars to travel very short journeys that are easy to walk;
- an understanding of the intensity and nature of the new friendships and the comparison of those with friendships at home;
- better relationships with siblings;
- a greater sense of personal and spiritual perspectives on life;
- a sense of service and giving;
- a change of self-concept.

Adapted from Allison, 2000: 71–77

Edventure all at sea: a tall-ship experience: by Chris Biggins, commander, Shabab Oman

Shabab Oman is the tall ship of Oman, the only Arab country to use sail training as an experiential learning platform. The ship, a 52-metre barquentine, was purchased second-hand in 1977 and had previously been the *Captain Scott*.

She was built in Buckie, Scotland by Herd and MacKenzie and commanded by Victor Clarke, who also skippered the Gordonstoun School vessel, *Prince Louis*, and therefore has a lineage with the principles of outward bound and Kurt Hahn.

The role: *Shabab Oman* commenced sail training in Oman in 1978, providing adventure training in groups of 24 from the armed forces of Oman. She has continued steadfast in this role for 27 years and to date some 600 trainees have passed through the ship. The basic concept is to provide sail and adventurous training, using the medium of the sea to develop personal skills, leadership potential and to foster teamwork. This in turn recalls Oman's long seafaring traditions and instils a link with history while pitting participants against the present-day challenges of the sea to deliver a powerful learning experience.

The experiential training concept: Trainees embark for a period of three weeks when the ship is operating on the coast of Oman and for up to four months when the ship deploys abroad. The trainee group consists of a mix of all branches of the armed forces, police and occasionally civilians. The group works and lives together within the confines of a sailing ship and they learn basic elements of seamanship and navigation while developing life skills of team working, problem solving and leadership. The idea of using the sea as a levelling medium from which to launch an experiential learning programme is not new and yet it possesses the potential to quickly reveal a person's inner strengths and weaknesses. The sea provides an ever-changing and challenging environment, which pits man against an unrelenting, unforgiving and formidable opponent. Trainees develop self-confidence through the successful completion of previously inconceivable tasks, working at height and in atrocious weather conditions, which infuse an enduring sense of achievement and often greatly enhanced self-esteem.

Micro hike

Journeys can take the form of detailed micro-hikes over a few metres of the floor of a forest or the circumference of a tree. Journeys can involve an orienteering exercise, or they can involve simply getting objects or people from A to B. They can be metaphorical, in thought only. Journeys can also be solely in the mind, and these form the basis of guided fantasy work in learning and therapy.

 ## Resources required

These activities can require extensive planning and health and safety assessments and checks.

See the following organizations for edventure ideas:

- Greenforce.
- Frontier.
- Earthwatch.
- RSPB.
- National Trust.
- BTCV.

Tip

Plan well in advance – but allow for some spontaneity and spontaneous emergent learning!

References and further reading

Allison, P (2000) Research from the ground up, *Brathay Occasional Papers*, **1**, Brathay Hall Trust, Cumbria

Beard, C and Wilson, J (2006) *Experiential Learning: A Best Practice Handbook for Educators and Trainers*, 2nd edn, Kogan Page, London

James, T (1995) Kurt Hahn and the aims of education, in (eds) K Warren, M Sakofs and J S Hunt *The Theory of Experimental Education*, pp 33–44, Kendall/Hunt Publishing Company, Dubuque, IA

Megginson, D (1994) Planned and emergent learning: a framework and a method, *Executive Development*, **7** (6), pp 29–32, MCB University Press, Manchester

Swarbrooke, J, Beard, C, Leckie, S and Pomfret, G (2003) *Adventure Tourism: The new frontier*, Butterworth-Heinemann, Oxford

See also my chapter on wildlife adventure tourism and artificial adventure tourism in Swarbrooke *et al* (2003).

See the very creative work on dramaturgy in Martin *et al* (2004) *Outdoor and Experiential Learning: An Holistic Approach to Programme Design*, Gower, Aldershot.

Different ways to know: spatial mapping of knowledge

What it achieves

This illustrative experience explores the relationships between space and knowledge. The experience focuses on the movement of knowledge within a space. The movement results in a new perspective, enabling information to be reformulated and reframed so that it can be seen differently.

This kind of experience of moving information is seen on films such as *Minority Report* and detective-style films that use technologically enhanced glass surfaces to view data and analyse them in different ways.

This experience provides an experiential substitute for speaking (using mostly verbal memory) or reading about specific information, or showing a lengthy and protracted PowerPoint® presentation.

Underlying principles

This activity illustrates the spatial reorganization of visual and non-visual data as an analytical tool. The spatial movement is both vertical and horizontal. The mapping of data in these two directions leads to the generation of different ways of seeing and knowing.

Specifically in connection with space, the illustrative technique outlined below focuses on visual memory images, using laminated photographs collected over many years around the globe. The images are of a diverse range of learning environments. Visual acuity and visual literacy support the development of new analytical skills: the subject under scrutiny can be seen in many different ways and so it is more deeply understood.

The experience develops an active approach to the engagement of learning materials rather than a passive viewing of multiple images. The activity develops higher levels of analysis and critical thinking using spatial reorganization of information, and the primary focus is on visual as well as auditory memory.

Specifically the experience focuses on the development of the following three forms of higher cognitive (mental) processing:

1. Analysis – select, compare, differentiate, contrast, break down.
2. Synthesis – summarize, argue, relate, precis, organize, generalize, conclude.
3. Evaluation – judge, evaluate, select, recognize, criticize.

The session develops the following skills essential in the development of critical thinking:

● the use of simple tools for critical analysis;
● the use of conceptualizing strategies and pattern detection (mind mapping, strengths and weaknesses, clustering, identifying frequency of occurrence of themes, synthesis and critical evaluation);
● the development of debating and discussion skills.

How to run it

On a large table, place the printed and laminated visual images (see Figure 1.4.1). This activity uses the topic of learning environments as illustrative only. The images in this experience include both outdoor and indoor environments for learning taken from around the world. The images might include artificial adventure caves made from shipping containers in Singapore, simple caves made from tyres, climbing towers, a paradise island, an infinity leisure pool in Dubai where the pool appears to merge with the natural sea, classrooms, informal learning spaces such as connecting spaces to classrooms being used by students in university, stand-up fast-food and computer malls developed in what were unused spaces in university corridors, and so forth.

Participants are asked to look for patterns, to sort, classify, organize and then debate and discuss a conceptual framework to classify these images.

Figure 1.4.1   *Learners exploring visual data (oil company staff, India)*

Various triggers can be suggested to assist the learning, as follows:

- Trends: large arrows made from cut-out card and laminated. These are used for identifying chronological–historical trends or design trends, where the arrows can signify direction and change.
- Clusters: the moving of data material can help with clustering or classification. This concerns the basic level of the organizing of visual images.
- Clusters of clusters: if we put a number of clusters of visual images together we may also be able to develop a meta-level of clustering or classification.
- Analytical commentaries: small cards with analytical commentary are placed next to the images by different people.

Some of the initial categories that can be created for the visual images include those shown in Table 1.4.1.

Table 1.4.1   *Learning spaces: towards a classification*

Micro – floor tiles	Macro – classroom
Real	Virtual
Underground	Land
Land	Sea
Artificial structures	Natural structures
Floor	Ceiling
Public spaces	Private spaces
Indoor	Outdoor
Doing spaces	Thinking spaces
Own	Groups
Creative spaces	Traditional spaces
Cafés	Libraries
Reading spaces	Thinking spaces
Talking spaces	Quiet 'solo' spaces
Combative (battling with nature)	Empathetic to nature

This analysis and synthesis can be continued to a next level so as to develop conceptual thinking and propositional knowledge.

 Resources required

● Large table (floor space can be used).
● Packs of printed images (laminated if to be used regularly).

Tips

Instead of using laminated photographs, stick-it labels can also be used to allow the possibilities of movement of information (see Figure 1.4.2).

This experience can also be used with non-visual material such as the analysis of 'critical incidents'. These can be learning incidents or difficult social interactions. The incident forms the base layer to a mapping approach. The base layer is thus an everyday interpretation of events that will lend themselves to a more detailed exploration.

Figure 1.4.2   *Stick-it labels permit movement of data and clustering but can easily fall off the wall surface after a while*

The next layer of analysis is generated from detailed group discussion, and the discussion continues through a number of layers, each one being the subject of a higher level of analysis. The work will lead to a deep group analysis of value-based decisions and ethical behaviour. A number of critical incidents can also be examined in this way by vertical and horizontal mapping.

For a good sample of critical incidents that occur in outdoor learning, see *Outdoor Experiential Leadership: Scenarios Describing Incidents, Dilemmas and Opportunities* by Tom Smith and Pete Allison (2006). This book has a useful synopsis of the scenarios, which can form the base layer for a much broader vertical and horizontal analysis of outdoor critical incidents. One example of the 62 presented in the book is 'They're having a "thing"'. In this exercise people attending a sea-kayaking course become aware of a developing affair between one of their peers and one of their instructors. One of the students has strong feelings about the inappropriateness of their actions, and is confused about how to act on his feelings. The ensuing group discussion develops a variety of possible solutions about these critical incidents. The solutions can then be moved around so that they too can be the basis of analysis, synthesis and evaluation.

References and further reading

Bass, B S (1956) *Taxonomy of Education: The Classification of Educational Goals*, Longman, London

Jensen, E (2000) *Brain-based Learning: The New Science of Teaching and Training*, The Brain Store, San Diego CA

Smith, T and Allison, P (2006) *Outdoor Experiential Leadership: Scenarios Describing Incidents, Dilemmas and Opportunities*, Learning Unlimited Publishing, Tulsa, OK and Racoon Institute Publications, Lake Geneva, WI

Listening to silence: experiencing silence through sensory focus

What it achieves

This experience utilizes outer space and silence to access the inner space of the self.

This experience concerns the ability to think about thinking and to become aware about being aware. This learning experience is about cultivating a degree of inner presence and the ability to work creatively with 'no mind' states.

Getting a sense of our outer or inner 'being' is a tall order for most people. Given the pace of life today, our minds are full of the incessant chattering of our inner voices about the future and the past. The introductory activities described below are unsophisticated and can be variously used to develop a new relationship with space and place.

The experiences, through connecting the inner spaces of the mind to the outer environment, develop a stillness for deep self-reflection in the moment of the here and now.

Underlying principles

Quiet time and quiet places are the antithesis of active experiential learning. The experience can be conducted as a solitary or solo experience, or as a group 'being alone together'. The experience involves having specific unhurried experiences in particular places and spaces. These experiences can have a profound effect on our sense of being, and can result in a heightened consciousness. These experiences avoid learning by active thinking and doing, or learning by getting or knowing. This is a break from the more traditional approaches to learning and so forms the last illustrative experience in this dimension that looks at the outer learning environment of space and place, nature and people.

It is important in this experience to reduce the inner chatter of the mind and to develop quiet, almost no-mind states. A no-mind state can be generated by shifting to what might be regarded as a mindless activity, a concept that is explored below. A reflective or meditative space emerges in one's self that is a potent form of learning, allowing deeper thinking about the 'here and now experience'. This experience can also open up space for new thinking, in a deeply reflective way, about very challenging situations we face in life.

Gerard Egan in *The Skilled Helper* (2002: 19) talks about the common-sense wisdom in the helping professions and suggests that 'Helpers need to be wise, and part of their job is to impart some of their wisdom, however indirectly, to their clients.' He then says that a number of authors have defined wisdom as 'an expertise in the conduct and meaning of life' or 'an expert knowledge system concerning the fundamental pragmatics of life'. He then asks what it is that characterizes wisdom and he offers some possibilities:

- Meta-thinking, or the ability to think about thinking and become aware about being aware.

This one statement I have deliberately singled out for this experiential approach to developing a sense of inner being, and the desire to develop wisdom.

The rest of the list comprises:

- Self-knowledge and maturity.
- Knowledge of life's obligations and goals.
- An understanding of cultural conditioning.
- The guts to admit mistakes and the sense to learn from them.
- A psychological and a human understanding of others; insight into human interactions.
- The ability to 'see through' situations; the ability to understand the meaning of events.
- Tolerance for ambiguity and the ability to work with it.
- Being comfortable with messy and ill-structured cases.

- An understanding of the messiness of human beings.
- Openness to events that do not fit comfortably into logical or traditional categories.
- The ability to frame a problem so that it is workable; the ability to reframe information.
- Avoidance of stereotypes.
- Holistic thinking; open-mindedness; open-endedness; contextual thinking.
- The ability to see relationships among diverse factors; the ability to spot flaws in reasoning; intuition; the ability to synthesize.
- The refusal to let experience become a liability through the creation of blind spots.
- The ability to take a long view of the problem.
- The ability to blend seemingly antithetical helping roles – being one who cares and understands while being also the one who challenges and 'frustrates'.
- An understanding of the spiritual dimensions of life.

In working with this internal chatter of our mind as it relates to our anxieties is the research by Albert Ellis, the founder of rational-emotional behaviour therapy (REBT). Ellis claims that one of the most useful interventions helpers can make is to challenge irrational beliefs, engaged in through self-talk.

Typical of these beliefs is that we believe we must:

- Be liked and loved. We must always be loved and approved by significant people in our life.
- Be competent. I must always, in all situations, demonstrate competence, and I must be both talented and competent in some important area of life.
- Have one's own way.
- Avoid being hurt.
- Be danger free.
- Be problemless.

This is the stuff of the chatter of our inner voice or voices. These are the voices that incessantly worry about the past and the future. In this way the voices encourage us to avoid being present in the here and now. Thus we become absent from our very own inner being. Thus we are not conscious of ourselves, and so we do not often think about our thinking, or become aware about being aware.

How to run it

Here four introductory experiences are introduced. The first involves developing a meditative state by simply focusing on a circle. The second idea involves the act of watching the fire in the outdoors. The third suggestion involves repetitive, routine and mindless physical exercise such as plodding the hills, swimming lengths, pushing a lawnmower or ironing up and down. Finally, other meditative possibilities are explored.

As a preliminary exercise read the following:

After the hurricane...

People had to walk to their jobs, and to whatever shops were still open. We began encountering each other on the streets, 'in person' instead of by telephone. In the absence of automobiles, and their loud engines, the rhythms of crickets and birdsong became clearly audible. Flocks of birds were migrating south for the winter, and many of us found ourselves simply listening with new and childlike curiosity to the ripples of song in the still-standing trees and the fields. And at night the sky was studded with stars! Many children, their eyes no longer blocked by the glare of houselights and street lamps, saw the Milky Way for the first time, and were astonished. For those few days and nights our town became a community aware of its place... The breakdown of our technologies had forced us to return to our senses, and hence to the natural landscape in which those senses are so profoundly embedded. We suddenly found ourselves inhabiting a sensuous world that had been waiting, for years, at the very fringe of our awareness, an intimate terrain...

Abram, 1997: 62

Ask people to initially become more aware of their sensory experiences, of their feelings and their mind states. This is the groundwork required to get to no-mind states.

Focusing on the circle: experiencing calm

Make yourself comfortable; find your own place to lie or sit relaxed with your hands down by your side or clasped on your lap.

Read these instructions once and then proceed to experience the activity for yourself.

Concentrate on the large circle in Figure 1.5.1 and take three minutes to listen to your own breathing.

Figure 1.5.1   *Focusing on the circle: experiencing calm*

Now concentrate on the exact middle of the circle; do not take your eyes off the circle, and use only your peripheral vision to slowly stimulate your senses by:

- seeing three objects around you;
- hearing three sounds;
- smelling three things;
- feeling three things.

You might have a slight feeling of an out-of-body experience. Now, empty the mind by not thinking, sensing or feeling. Just sit and be...

Sitting together watching the fire

Here it is important to allow time to be with one other person by a real fire in the outdoors, and to have periods where there is silence and no one talks. Places allowing panoramic views help, as do rivers or lakes. It is the same as the exercise above and the increased awareness of the senses can act as a preliminary activity to experiencing a no-mind state. Here, though, there is an emphasis on being alone together (Nicolls *et al*, 2008).

Repetitive, routine physical exercise

Encourage yourself to take opportunities and space to walk alone, to swim alone, to 'be' alone to wander in hotel grounds or to plod the surrounding hills – alone. Even if space is limited it is important to create personal time for ruminative reflective mind states. These activities can also divert the tendency to socialize on learning and development programmes through eating food and drinking caffeine and alcohol: not always the best option to create space learning.

Pressures of life prevent us finding these times in everyday-life situations, as we need to find time for socializing, for children, to go on holidays, to cook, to do the garden and see to household chores, with lawns to mow and ironing to do. But these things are also opportunities… to prepare the ground so we can stop for a while to just experience 'being'. The lawn mowing and ironing are different: they are deliberately selected as they have great potential to become 'mindless' activities. Practise rhythmic routine jobs as meditative activities, to empty the mind.

While doing any of these routine activities, listen to your own voice as a first step. Mentally record yourself talking to yourself. Decide if it is about pleasurable things, about worries, money, children, etc. We need to work towards silencing these voices for longer and longer periods and just 'be', if we can, to empty out our mind in order to create space for nothingness, and it can seem hard to do at times.

Develop meditative states

Meditative states are not always as they appear in the books. While talking to a Chinese Confucian philosopher a group of people remarked how they wished they could meditate. One person told him that they could easily stare at the view through their lounge and kitchen at home, and just admire the things that they could see. This they could do for half an hour or more when they were on their own. They said they just seemed to enjoy the beauty of a view through the rooms and out into the garden. The Confucian philosopher said that this was a natural meditation, leading to a no-mind state. This person then gave up reading books on meditation!

These dimensions of experience involve just being and the experience is only concerned with the formless; it is not of or about 'things'.

Indeed Socrates described wisdom as not knowing.

 **Resources required**

● Very little!

Identify beforehand some good places for being alone.
Create safe outdoor log fires or use a barbeque.

Tip

Ask people to get into the habit of doing this regularly by themselves, either alone or with others. This might be a brief moment in the shower in the morning, or in the gym or swimming pool. Exercise can also link mind and body, and health and well-being, so as to create a stronger life balance and so link this to these deeper reflective states.

 References and further reading

Abram, D (1997) *The Spell of the Sensuous*, Vintage Books, New York
Egan, G (2002) *The Skilled Helper: a problem-management and opportunity-development approach to helping*, Brooks/Cole Publishing, Pacific Grove CA
Nicolls, R *et al* (2008) Busy doing nothing: researching the phenomenon of quiet time in outdoor experiential learning, paper presented at ICEL, Sydney, December 2008
See also books or tapes by Eckhart Tolle.

Part 2

The second dimension: doing

Introduction

Focus

- Understanding the practical issues of what the learners do in order to learn.
- The important practice question here is: What is it that learners are actually going to do?

Do we have to actually do something in order to learn experientially? The word 'doing' does have connotations of being active, but doing of course does not necessarily mean being physically active: ideally, experiential learning actively engages the whole person. Learning involves expressing and receiving (symbolic/language) information that is used to represent our world, by various means such as drawing, reading, writing, listening and talking These are also forms of doing. Furthermore, it has often been assumed that 'doing the real thing' is also a central tenet of experiential learning – but what do we mean when we suggest that it is best to learn by doing the 'real' thing? These issues are addressed in practice in this section.

The degree to which a learning activity is real, or at least perceived as real, and the extent to which this reality is manipulated by educators or trainers, is a key consideration in experiential learning. The degree of realness of the activity is certainly an important theoretical and practical consideration in learner engagement. Pilots, for example, learn to fly through the use of complex flight simulators. Whether the learning concerns philosophy or tree felling, the experience will rarely start with the complexity of the whole picture. Tree felling, for example, does not start with large trees and chainsaws:

beginners start with small trees and bowsaws to learn the basic techniques first. There is usually a shift from simplicity to complexity, and within this shift the degree of perceived 'realness' and richness of the experience are two of the most important ingredients of learning activities. The subject of 'realness' receives a whole chapter of its own in Beard and Wilson (2006).

The degree to which a learner perceives an activity as real can vary depending on a number of key dimensions of the experience, including, for example, how real the actual task is, how real the environment is, how real the artefacts are and so forth. While a learning activity might be experienced as only a game or recreational or adventurous type of activity, the behaviours such as communication, team working or leadership exhibited by people during the activity, and later reflected upon, can of course be very real.

So-called 'real' projects or learning activities might also include real environmental or community projects for the purpose of providing a learning task. These kinds of learning tasks, often known as service learning activities, can generate very real environmental or community benefits. Real problems and real research issues are prevalent in experiential approaches to learning.

Many indoor and outdoor learning activities appear to consist of a number of common ingredients or design principles. They will have aspects of intellectual, physical and emotional engagement: this is because providing a balanced challenge is often a key to engagement and successful learning. Repeating a lot of low-level physical activities can often involve minimal levels of mental stimulation: they can get boring after a while. Mind, heart and body (ie cognitive, affective and kinaesthetic) experiences might, for example, include the building of a complex structure, perhaps with limited resources, or the management of a virtual organization, the solving of complex problems or researching a topic.

Sometimes the activity involves a journey, which may be geographical, imaginary or chronological. Most, if not all, activities involve obstacles and problems that must be overcome by the participants. These may be real or imaginary, and require those involved to operate within an agreed set of rules. New obstacles may be introduced, rules altered and targets changed depending upon the learning aims and objectives. These basic ingredients derived from a wide range of learning activities are discussed and explored in detail in Chapter 5 of Beard and Wilson (2006) and a 17-point checklist of such principles is outlined again there. The list can be added to by ongoing experiences, as it is not intended to be exhaustive or definitive. While each of the 17 basic ingredients will receive attention in various parts of this book, the Bike it! exercise is particularly focused on experiences of all these ingredients in one exercise, and has the 17-point learning typology reproduced within it.

A myriad of dichotomies all have to be considered in the design process as balance is very much the watchword: stories and journeys, planned and unplanned learning, reality versus simulation, written and visual, objects to help and objects as obstacles. Sequencing, pacing and the management of challenge and support are all covered throughout the activities in this book.

Scope of Part 2

Five main activities are presented in Part 2. In order to gain a more complete understanding of the doing dimension, all five illustrative experiences are briefly explained below.

✓ Experience 2.1: Bike it!

This experience focuses on the conceptual area of active doing, in this case constructing objects, in order to learn. Here there is a key concept to consider: that of the relationship between a simulated experience and a real experience. This activity details how many elements of doing can then be made more or less difficult in that a facilitator uses, in a metaphorical sense, 'control buttons' that can turn the degree of pressure up or down, obstacles to make the exercise more difficult, or they can alter income generation or financial accountability. The experience highlights how any simple structure, such as a raft, bike, jigsaw, a banquet, chocolate making, a poem or a theory can all be broken down into their smaller components for the learners to then rebuild. In this case a simple children's bike is broken down or deconstructed for the learners to rebuild or reconstruct.

✓ Experience 2.2: Altering reality

This experience involves learning negotiating by doing real negotiating, but the experience illustrates how elements of perceived or actual reality can be subtly altered within a learning activity. The concept of altering dimensions of realness can be applied to almost any kind of training, from communication skills development and sales training to flying and sailing skills. The use of real artefacts (eg cars, documents), to aid learning, is also illustrated in this experience.

✓ Experience 2.3: Read all about them

This experience involves the development of writing skills. The experience focuses on 'doing' writing, whether for company reports or MBA assignments.

Report writing is a difficult skill to master. Knowing how to write is as important as knowing what to write. This learning activity looks at experiential skills development for writing introductions and conclusions and focuses on the mobility and manipulation of information, moving through a sequence of activities from simple simulation to more complex and real experiences.

✓ *Experience 2.4: Antiques Roadshow*

This experience develops product awareness in groups of people through the process of learning by doing, as in thinking aloud when describing objects or products. The learners might be apprentices, volunteers or experienced sales staff. In speaking about and handling a variety of selected products, knowledge unfolds through sensing (the touch, feel and sound of products as sensory experiences), and through careful observation that builds on existing experiences. This fun and adaptable sensory approach generates a deeper commercial knowledge, increases confidence and awareness of company product functions and variable costs about anything from mobile phones to tools and equipment.

✓ *Experience 2.5: Hearing voices*

This experience focuses on learning by doing as in the multiple analyses of conversations or discourse. The context is customer-service training, involving call-centre and reception staff training. This experience offers a creative way to develop learner-centred approaches to voice training, customer-care skills and dealing with difficult customers. Learning and change occur in the training session and the transformation can be easily nurtured and developed.

A range of other concepts to work on in the doing dimension

1. Move gradually from simple activities to more complex problem-solving and/or research-type experiences as learning activities.

2. Start with known popular activities from the world of the learner and move to the more complex unknown activities. Stepping the learning in stages and constructing key learning issues, outdoor facilitators might consider chocolate making if they always do raft building, tank driving and the like. Coffee and papers is a good solo-plus-collaborative exercise, while research

might look at the well-known claim about 'a glass and a half of milk in every bar of chocolate'!

3. Consider how different learning environments suit different learning activities.

4. Do not concentrate on one mode for too long. Be aware of balance as a design concept (using body, cognition, emotion). Mind, body and heart need to be engaged in learning to varying degrees.

5. Give shape, sequence, flow and form to the learning journey.

6. In the journey from simple to complex, from known to unknown, incorporating high or low levels of simulation to higher or lower levels of reality that can be stepped down (role play with masks, fantasy, etc) or stepped up (flight simulators).

7. Consider the degree of reality of the task, the processing and the environment that the learning is located in (natural, artificial, virtual, etc), as well as the degree of reality of the people and artefacts, etc.

8. Simulations can also go beyond reality, by using augmented reality.

9. Deconstruction in design then allows learners to reconstruct; this is an important principle in experiential design.

10. Use the 17-point typology below as metaphorical volume-control knobs that can be used by facilitators and learners to increase the levels of difficulty or complexity, time, money, constraints, problems, etc. This typology was developed by examining some of the most frequently applied themes regularly present in learning activities.

11. Consider the balance of collaboration and competition.

12. Digital capturing devices enable, for example, visual and auditory data to be used, alongside editing technologies, for learner feedback and learner-generated materials development.

13. Learners can be both consumers and producers of knowledge.

A learning experience might include:

1. Setting a target, goal or objective, where goals create an underlying state of mind.

2. Creating a sense of a journey or destination – physical movement and exercise; people, information and objects are moved from A to B.

3. Allowing participants to exercise many forms of intelligence.

4. Creating and sequencing a theme of social, mental, psychological and physical activities – mind, spirit and body.

5. Adjusting elements of reality.

6. Stimulating multiple senses.

7. Using a concept of construction or deconstruction in activity design: a physical object, eg bike, wall or raft, or a non-physical item, eg a clue, phrase or poem.

8. Designing in social collaborative or competitive strategies.

9. Creating combative and/or empathetic approaches to the environment.

10. Creating restrictions:
    – obstacles;
    – sensory blocking, eg blindfolds;
    – rules;
    – procedures.

11. Providing elements of real or perceived challenge or risk.

12. Setting time constraints.

13. Allowing people to deal with change, risk, success and failure – stretching personal boundaries.

14. Designing, sorting and/or organization skills – a mass of data or information to sort, or activities to do or consider.

15. Functional skills such as surveying, juggling, map reading, knot tying, etc.

16. Designing quiet time for reflection – physical or mental space.

17. Allowing the reflective story of the experience to be told.

 **Reference**

Beard, C and Wilson, J P (2006) *Experiential Learning: A Best Practice Handbook for Educators and Trainers*, 2nd edn, Kogan Page, London

Bike it!: teams, leadership and communication

What it achieves

Bike it! is a fun exercise involving groups of people actively doing things together. The doing involves the construction of an object; in this case a bicycle is illustratively used by blending both indoor and outdoor experiences. Other objects can be used.

The activity can be designed to test, explore and develop a range of broad and narrow skills. Broad skills include, for example, team working, decision making, leadership, communication or financial skills.

The activity also builds in an extensive range of narrow skills such as the management of basic accounts, currency conversion, problem solving to earn money; and numerous other core skills that embrace the cognitive, physical and emotional domains can be designed into the event.

Problem solving is tested to the extreme, using a complex multiple set of experiences in a range of learning environments.

Underlying principles

This approach to learning uses the simple design concept where a facilitator deconstructs an object. The learner, of course, has to reverse this and so (re) construct the object.

A bike or model helicopter or similar physical structure – or non-physical structures – can all be broken down or deconstructed into their constituent parts and these become objects that form the basis of subsequent complex design principles. In this example people collect parts, buy parts, build parts and find parts in order to (re)build a complete functional working object.

In parallel with this deconstruction approach, the trainer or educator also breaks down the skills that are required for the learning programme, eg teamwork or decision making.

For example, communication can be broken down into listening, speaking, questioning, articulation and precision, etc.

Broad skills can thus be broken down into a narrower subset of skills. In this way complex skills can be cumulatively developed during the experience, having been built into the experience of the various learning activities. Many activities can of course be incorporated into the construction of a bike. It is better if the activities are very varied in nature; this allows learners more opportunities to test and work with their strengths or to test weaker areas. Activities thus need to provide physical, emotional and intellectual challenge, memorizing and so forth. The activities can also include a certain degree of risk taking and time or decision-making pressure.

Figure 2.1.1   *Experiential activity can use the principle of deconstruction and reconstruction of a physical object*

Activities might include cryptic clues to solve, logical problems to crack, visual-acuity tasks such as 'photofit' activities or photo orienteering, or the carrying out of physical tasks requiring accuracy, such as target shooting, or involving the purchase of arrows, balls or balloons (see below for further explanations of this repertoire of activities). Investment opportunities might involve a degree of financial risk, involving decision making and risk assessment. A bike shop may open at certain times and allow opportunities to purchase tools and bike parts. All these activities can be regulated with rules or procedures and time constraints so as to make activities more or less difficult.

Competitive or collaborative strategies can be applied using more than one team focused on the building of the bike(s).

A basic learning activity design brief consisting of the 17 principles (the typology) given in the Introduction can be applied to add to the design complexity.

The design principle here then is that any physical structure – or indeed a non-physical structure such as a theory or poem – could be used for this learning activity.

How to run it

Bike it! was initially designed by final-year university students who were very experienced mountain-bike cyclists; they were themselves competent in bike construction and maintenance. Their course module focused on the design of complex outdoor activities for management development.

The learning activity typology below is taken from the sister book, *Experiential Learning: A Best Practice Handbook for Educators and Trainers* by Colin Beard and John P Wilson (2006). In this book a range of additional design principles are highlighted for use in experiential learning.

The principles listed here as a typology form the basic design brief:

1. Setting a target, goal or objective, where goals create an underlying state of mind.
2. Creating a sense of a journey or destination – physical movement and exercise; people, information and objects are moved from A to B.
3. Allowing participants to exercise many forms of intelligence.
4. Creating and sequencing a theme of social, mental, psychological and physical activities – mind, spirit and body.
5. Adjusting elements of reality.
6. Stimulating multiple senses.

7. Using a concept of construction or deconstruction in activity design: a physical object, eg bike, wall or raft, or a non-physical item, eg a clue, phrase or poem.

8. Designing in social collaborative or competitive strategies.

9. Creating combative and/or empathetic approaches to the environment.

10. Creating restrictions:
    - obstacles;
    - sensory blocking, eg blindfolds;
    - rules;
    - procedures.

11. Providing elements of real or perceived challenge or risk.

12. Setting time constraints.

13. Allowing people to deal with change, risk, success and failure – stretching personal boundaries.

14. Designing, sorting and/or organization skills – a mass of data or information to sort, or activities to do or consider.

15. Functional skills such as surveying, juggling, map reading, knot tying, etc.

16. Designing quiet time for reflection – physical or mental space.

17. Allowing the reflective story of the experience to be told.

This set of principles originated from a detailed analysis of over 300 basic outdoor learning activities. They evolved from an attempt to tease out and identify the common ingredients that were often built into such outdoor activities.

The basic idea of this learning activity is that a bike is deconstructed into its most basic parts (two bikes if two teams are competing). The handlebars and two wheels are first separated from the frame. The frame, wheels and handlebars are hidden in the outdoors and form the locations for orienteering exercises (in this specific case we used a national park location). Difficult cryptic clues are used for the route map that assisted discovery of their whereabouts. Grid reference numbers are included but on their own they do not disclose the precise location – further systematic team searches were still required.

The bike clearly could not be built without these core components and the solution required a systematic search involving a few allocated/designated people from the team who were prepared to engage with considerable physical activity.

By carrying out many smaller activities (see below), team members could all generate funds by applying differing skills (money in different currencies – euros, dollars, etc). Other basic bike parts could then be purchased at a simulated bike shop, which might only open at specified times. A fully completed bike is not required to conclude the task as the objective is that it must be demonstrated that it can be ridden safely for 20 metres. Parts and tools could both be purchased but no guarantee applied for some parts (they did not work or were unsuitable) as they were second-hand and bought 'as seen'. Bike-building expertise might also be purchased – an investment.

The variable sums of money earned by completing the range of tasks have to be accounted for at any time. The set of accounts can be presented in the home-nation currency, and might be required to be available for inspection at any time. Currency conversion might also be required at times to assess the international currency value. Fines could result from a failure to make appropriate accounts available at specified times.

Some learning activities might require an initial investment by the team, in order to generate larger sums of money in return; however, these might require an element of financial risk.

The tasks involved varying levels of competition and collaboration. Some tasks required only one person to solve, others required more people to achieve. Some activities were virtually impossible to achieve and were potentially time wasting for team members if engaged with. Some required innovative solutions (a hot bacon sandwich was specified for a sum of money and one student group found some old bacon in the bins from breakfast in the residential centre and heated it in the microwave and presented it – the rules did not say it had to be edible!). Some tasks involved the completion of jigsaw designs of the major theories from their lectures (revision skills built into these exercises).

Tasks usually required supervisors to watch, sign off and award funds for each activity; the tutors had to be booked at specific times.

Well-known tasks included blindfold tent erection, spider's web, and shepherd and sheep. Others were newly created – such as the presentation of a valid train ticket for that day (the station was several miles away but the money that could be earned was considerable).

Activities might include visual acuity, using photofit pictures where money can be earned by finding and matching a set of photographs in a specified surrounding area, thus testing powers of observation.

Sample activity descriptions

Cryptic clues

A typical example of this kind of activity might be to make a list of simple cryptic clues. They might be as follows:

Value £1 each: easier clues:

11 p... in a cricket t...;
365 d... in a y...;
8 p... in a g... .

Value £2 each: slightly harder clues:

22 b... o... a s... t...;
1,609 m... in a m... .

The answers are:

11 players in a cricket team;
365 days in a year;
8 pints in a gallon;
22 balls on a snooker table;
1,609 metres in a mile.

Another variation would be to develop a list of items that must be found for the value of £3; for example:

Something to make you cry (answer: an onion);
A picture of the Queen (answer: £20 note);
A bunch of dates (answer: a diary).

Logical/mathematical

A range of design ideas for these activities can be found in the little booklets on sale in newsagents. They often have the description 'logic problems' on the front cover. The classic problem of this kind would involve, for example, the following information:

> Three business executives left the airport at different times on the same morning on the way to long-haul-destination meetings. From the clues given below you must establish the details of who caught which flight, what their full name was and at what time they flew.

1. The flight to Sydney had the next take-off time after Andrew's plane.
2. Gemma was multiple to 940 flight.
3. The passenger named Freddie to the plane which left 920.
4. The ticket for New York was held by Nancy, who is not Claire.

Similar logical exercises can easily be created.

Table 2.1.1   *A logical/mathematical problem*

	Freddie	Flemming	Nancy	Bangkok	Sydney	New York	9.20	9.30	9.40
Andrew									
Claire									
Gemma									
9.20									
9.30									
9.40									
Bangkok									
Sydney									
New York									

Answer

Freddie who was on the 9.20 flight (3) cannot have been going to Sydney (1) and Nancy was the passenger for New York (4), so Bangkok must have been Freddie's destination, which leaves Flemming as the passenger for Sydney. Neither Andrew (1) nor Gemma (2) took off at 9.40 so Claire must have done so. She was not going to New York (4) so her 9.40 flight must have been to Sydney, leaving 9.30 as the time for take-off for Nancy's New York flight. Now, from (1) Andrew must be Nancy who left at 9.30, leaving Gemma as Freddie, the 9.20 passenger for Bangkok. Therefore:

Andrew Nancy, New York, 9.30.
Claire Flemming, Sydney, 9.40.
Gemma Freddie, Bangkok, 9.20.

Financial

Each team can be provided with a basic starting sum of money. Simulated banknotes will need to be created for the purpose of this activity. Basic book-keeping skills can be introduced. The internet can provide up-to-date currency conversions so that financial figures can be presented in different international currencies. Currency rates can also be found within daily newspapers. Financial risk taking can be introduced by offering investment opportunities. The decision-making processes regarding the degree of difficulty of the task all require the financial return on investment of time to be taken into account as well as the skills available within the team conducting the problem.

More complex financial activity can be introduced using taxation. This might include introducing and changing VAT rates.

Visual acuity

For this type of activity photofit can be used whereby photographs of difficult-to-find images have to be perfectly matched. This can involve pictures within the building or in the outdoors. A typical example of a difficult image for hotel managers to find might include fire-prevention equipment with codes on, or drain covers with specific codes in the hotel grounds. To establish this activity as an investment opportunity the financial return on these images may be extremely high, but the team might have to purchase a camera, and each memory card would also cost a specific sum of money and have only a limited memory available.

Photographic orienteering exercises can also be introduced. Here photographic images provide the route to follow in order to discover a range of clues, numbers, colours or codes that, when pieced together, will enable the team to solve a complex problem with a significant financial return as a result.

Literacy and numeracy!

A very simple money-generating activity would be to provide the team with a set of large laminated A4 sheets with a number or a letter on each sheet. The team could be given five minutes' thinking time to choose either words or numbers and then within a specific and very limited time they would have to generate the maximum number of words from their laminated sheets of letters while being supervised in order to gain a financial return.

Alternatively, for numerical work they would have to generate the correct answer to a specified set of numbers using the following rules: six members of the team must take part and when asked to present their answer each member must have a card showing either a number or a plus, minus, divide or multiply symbol in front of them.

Physical

Stomp rockets or sling-type catapults with balloons can be used to test physical-kinaesthetic skills. These can be set up so that targets have to be hit by the rockets or balloons. This can represent a form of financial gamble, where funds can be effectively doubled. This investment, through the purchase of rockets or balloons, means that funds can go up as well as down depending on these physical skills.

Decision making

Clearly all these activities require teams to organize themselves in terms of the skills available, the distribution of human and financial resources, and the degree of certainty or otherwise of completing the task within specific time constraints. It is important that within the duration of this whole activity there are a large number of learning activities to complete that will test and develop a variety of skills and knowledge. The activities outlined above are merely illustrative and relatively simple. Much more complex tasks can be introduced towards the end of the activity. These complex tasks might relate to the development of codes and numbers, gained from simpler activities, in order to solve something much more complex.

 **Resources required**

- Two bikes.
- Spare bike parts, both suitable and unsuitable.
- Tools.
- Books for the presentation of accounts.
- Handouts with a list of all tasks and money available on completion.
- Simulated banknotes of varying value.

 Tips

This is an advanced version of using planks and drums to build a raft to get across a river. It can be designed with other objects besides bikes.
   This activity can also be based on:

- The designing, costing, and delivering of a banquet.
- The making of chocolates, including wrapping up, marketing, etc, has also been tried by some facilitators.

● The construction of a kit (helicopter or model).

● The design principle was further developed and successfully applied to the building of dry-stone walls in a UK national park with leading commercial organizations, Management development took place while large sections of walls in the national park were repaired! Thus the notion of environmental service learning was incorporated.

● This design idea was also adapted to experiential service learning using a menu of alternative environmental projects with the UK's largest map maker.

Tips on using rules and obstacles:

● These are important functions for adults and young people alike, and require careful consideration by providers. However, many other simple rules, obstacles or procedures can all influence the degree of adventure, challenge or difficulty of any experiential activity.

● These rules and obstacles can allow greater flexibility in a programme design so that the experience can be altered and levels of challenge can be reduced or increased.

● Time constraints might, for example, mean that items such as bike parts can only be purchased during specific times. Two-way radios can be used on certain frequencies; battery life can be measured or curtailed.

● Solar panels can be used to charge batteries or equipment so that people can carry out some tasks only when the sun is shining.

● Items can be placed in the way of routes and the journey might only be allowed at night or through certain territory.

● Instructions can be given on a tape recording through earplugs so that only one person can hear them at any one time. Communication might be restricted to coded whistles or translated into another language.

● Obstacles can include sensory deprivation or sensory adjustment, and might include blindfolds, earplugs, glasses to improve or remove vision, nose pegs, gloves to remove feeling or to create clumsiness or even cardboard tubes to create a form of tunnel vision.

● Tarpaulins can be used to separate teams and they might be allowed to pass items only through a narrow aperture. Sorting and organization skills are also important skills to develop: a mass of data, a mass of information to sort and make sense of, or activities to decide who and when. Why? Because knowledge is one thing; organized knowledge is a million things! The range of combinations increases the level of challenge. Whilst the range is endless, it does need a degree of focus, structure and reason.

Example: The following rules and restrictions apply!

1. The time limit to complete the activities is just 520 minutes.
2. Each activity can be completed only once and will earn you money.
3. Each activity requires you to estimate your projected earnings and to submit the estimate to the facilitator before commencing.
4. Physical activities will be paid in dollars; mental tasks will be paid in euros.
5. The four teams will have radio contact for 10 minutes only during each half-hour.
6. One team member must be blindfolded at all times. One person must wear gloves at all times. For blindfold and glove wearing, rotation of the wearers is allowed.
7. A sum of 10 dollars will be paid for each digital picture of the team completing an activity.
8. An up-to-date set of accounts must be ready for inspection at any time.
9. Teams A and B will submit a mind-map plan of their proposals to the facilitators before commencing.
10. Teams C and D will not be required to produce a plan.

 **Further reading**

Beard, C and Wilson, J (2006) *Experiential Learning: A Best Practice Handbook for Educators and Trainers*, 2nd edn, Kogan Page, London

Martin, A, Franc, D and Zounkova, D (2004) *Outdoor and Experiential Learning: An Holistic and Creative Approach to Programme Design*, Gower, Aldershot

Neuman, J (2004) *Education and Learning through Outdoor Activities*, Duha, Czech Republic

Altering reality: negotiating skills development

What it achieves

This experience is an active, experiential and hands-on approach to the development of negotiating skills. The focus is on a range of ideas for actively doing negotiating.

Underlying principles

This activity uses a stepped or sequenced approach to the gradual increase in the degree of reality of the experience. The experience thus gradually exposes the learner to increased levels of realness in terms of moving towards the type of negotiating in which learners are actually involved on a day-to-day basis. This activity uses negotiation as illustrative to highlight the experiential concept of altering levels of 'realness' of the experience. By doing this, confidence can be gradually built; thus there is a link to the emotional dimension of learning.

Negotiating is considered a very complex or 'broad' skill, similar in many ways to competencies like team working, communication or leadership. Negotiating thus embraces many composite skills such as questioning, bargaining, diplomacy, influencing, persuasion, listening, tactics, entry, developing rapport, closing deals and so on. These subset skills have to be identified and understood within the skill of negotiating: they are developed and built upon through a range of sequenced experiences. These narrower skills have to be learnt first; thus the sequence and flow of the learning experience are particularly important.

As the 'narrow' skills are developed, opportunities are then provided for the learners to practise newly acquired skills within a context of low levels of reality. Gradually the broad complex skills are developed and the broader practice of negotiating is provided by raising the levels of reality and reducing the levels of simulation as shown below. There are, however, a number of dimensions of 'realness' in terms of the degree to which the task is perceived as real, or the degree to which the environment of the experience is perceived as real or not. Some experiences deliberately involve low levels of reality so that ultimately the learners can journey through dimensions of perceived reality as shown below.

How to run it

First an illustrative experiential activity is highlighted that has low content reality.

Illustrative exercise A: decorating the office

This is a simple textbook exercise from a standard training package on negotiating. It concerns agreeing the contract price to decorate an office. It can easily be created by trainers.

Learners are asked to read the brief and then identify and design opening gambits and write their answers only on paper. The subject of using opening gambits and pricing strategies could then be focused on and discussed with others on the course.

Illustrative exercise B: driving a bargain

This is a written exercise about car bargaining. People are asked to read the brief and are informed that this is a warm-up exercise in preparation for a more complex, real car-negotiating exercise, where they will be expected to pit their wits against real car-showroom negotiators. This exercise involves two cars that are different in their age, mileage, state of repair, etc, and a detailed report is included on each. The older car is to be traded in for the newer car. People are asked to prepare the main negotiating points they might use. This is then discussed to highlight potential learning points.

Illustrative exercise C: buying the car

Real cars are 'experienced' this time. Cars can be inspected in real life, and faults and advantages identified, both inside and outside, as they are both located outside in the car park. The participants receive car book prices and current car sales magazines to establish the general market prices. Participants are expected to negotiate with real people who are experienced car-sales negotiators. These negotiators are located in an office where the deals will take place. Final agreements are written in sealed envelopes so that the winners can be announced later.

A plenary discussion takes place as to the tactics used by the whole group. These are drawn up as guidelines.

Then move on to high content reality.

Illustrative exercise D: land access

This illustrative case here, highlighting the principles involved in moving towards the specific negotiating experiences that the learners seek to develop, is that of land-access negotiating. Here the experiential activities have to deliver an improved ability to negotiate with UK landowners for the right of the public to walk over land.

Access to land for public recreation is a complex business. Learners negotiate with landowners for access to farmland, moorland and mountains on behalf of the public. The landowners want money for such access. If learners are successful the public can then gain access via footpaths and other forms of land rights of passage. In the UK there are over 140,000 miles of footpath rights across the land.

In real life landowners ask agents to negotiate on their behalf. In one case of this exercise, an experienced land agent consented to help train the participants. Real trading information was generated based on his experience of how negotiations usually develop. Landowners, for example, negotiate using negative comments about things like gates left open, crop and wall damage and complex facts and figures about their financial losses, the need for grants, and sheep headage payments. They ask if they can have countryside ranger support from the government to keep people under control if needed.

For the participants the incentive is to try to do a good job in front of their peers. The exercise is recorded on video and they are given feedback. They are required to use the skills and knowledge acquired from less real scenarios so far provided on the course, and put these into practice. They are required first to study, and then to set out their own pre-set prices, subsidy targets and backstop strategies. These are decided in advance and declared in a recorded interview and their outline plans for negotiating are considered.

The groups negotiate and argue their case with the real land agent; debriefing takes place afterwards. Groups see who can make the 'best' deals.

The videos are replayed for self- and peer assessment and made available for participants at the end of the programme.

 ## Resources required

- Two cars owned by participants or facilitators in the car park.
- Car book price information.
- Current car sales magazines.
- Video and/or sound recording equipment.
- Experienced car-sales people.
- Experienced land agents.
- One simple written negotiation exercise.

Tips

Consider the training, for example, of a tree surgeon, a doctor or a pilot. This kind of training is used in emergency-forces training. The build-up that is required for such training leads to learning experiences that are very close to the real thing in order to avoid, for example, trauma when experiencing shocking scenes that they will eventually have to deal with.

This kind of design can also be used for many other skills training scenarios such as telephone training, doing presentations and so forth.

All such experiences can alter, ie raise or lower, dimensions of reality:

- people reality (a real pilot sitting next to the trainees);
- artefact reality (cockpit of the simulator);
- real skills (movement of the levers and control panels replicate the real thing);
- real mediating artefacts, such as cars;
- real environments, such as a car showroom.

The lowering of reality can include role plays, drama, dramaturgy, fantasy, the use of masks, all of which are explained briefly in Beard and Wilson (2006).

 **Further reading**

A chapter is devoted to altering reality in *Experiential Learning: A Best Practice Handbook for Educators and Trainers* by Colin Beard and John P Wilson (2006, Kogan Page, London).

Some interesting papers include 'Designed reality into management learning events' by D Binstead and R Stewart, published in *Personnel Review*, **8**, (3), (1979).

Read all about them: an experience to develop writing skills

What it achieves

The activity experientially develops the skills of writing introductions, conclusions, abstracts and executive summaries.

This activity improves the general development of writing skills for reports and other documented written material, including higher-degree-level work.

Underlying principles

The activity involves individual work, group work, competition and collaboration. The activity has a double benefit in that it experientially allows people to get to know each other while simultaneously learning to write introductions by doing them. A benefit of this activity is that it does not separate the time-consuming inductive 'getting to know' periods when a group first comes together from the development of writing skills.

This activity also demonstrates how to create a series of smaller building blocks of activity that develop more complex writing experiences.

This activity deliberately introduces participants to specific textbooks on writing skills so as to direct and develop the reading of the literature about writing skills development.

How to run it

Part one: the art of writing introductions

In this activity participants experience the skills required to write an introduction by first writing on an A4 page any information they want to divulge about themselves. They are asked to fill the whole page, if possible, and they are told that they can do this in any way they want to.

Note: if the idea of a 'life map' or life story filling a page is difficult for a particular group of people, then an alternative would be to fill a page with details of a hobby, a particular interest, favourite places, favourite television programmes or any other similar themes of personal interest.

Participants then find someone they do not know or do not know very well to work with. They greet, talk and then exchange their sheets of paper and talk about what they have written. This process of getting to know, and sharing stories with, another person for about a quarter of an hour can be an excellent icebreaker: thus the experience has a parallel purpose, which is to learn to write introductions about this new acquaintance as well as getting to know and experience them in person.

The participants then write a brief introduction to the page of personal details from this new acquaintance in no more than five or six sentences. This is often experienced as a difficult task despite its simplicity, but it stimulates awareness of the necessary skills required to write good introductions. This task often proves especially difficult for groups of lecturers from higher education! The focus is on the powers of observation in terms of what has been written and what has not been written and possibly how it has been written.

When most people have written an introduction they are encouraged to read aloud bits of their introductions to their colleagues. Discussion ensues about the writing of introductions and what is involved. It can lead to questions about general writing skills. The following questions may be useful prompts:

What did you find yourself doing in order to write a brief introduction?
What was it that the writing of this introduction has actually encouraged in terms of observation skills?

People often remark that they focused on the main elements, the essence, of the life story or life map presented to them. The introduction needs to succinctly cover the ground or territory without repeating the specific information, etc. Immediate observation might reveal that the story is divided into three or four sections, covering areas of a life such as family, career, etc. The ability to observe what is not covered can also be usefully explored.

The next activity involves a group approach to learning these skills rather than an individual task. This facilitates further discussion. This is a 'simulation' task that involves writing an introduction to a fictitious character as a person who has mapped out their life story in the form of a mind map. Each group works together at a table in order to collaboratively develop an introduction about this fictitious character. I have referred to this character below as Eric Jones. It can also be changed to Erica Jones, or alternatively a suggestion for this activity is that a new version of the mind-map story below is created such that it is more precisely suited to the group that is present.

Here a sense of fun and a degree of critical competitiveness are encouraged by allowing voting for the best effort. The competitiveness can be introduced by telling the group that they will also compete with voice recording of an introduction (one possible answer) developed by a previous group.

Task instructions

Write an introduction to the fictitious person, Eric (a low-level simulation of a piece of writing that is presented in this case as a mind map; see below).

1. Work in pairs or threes.
2. Start the assignment with 'Eric Jones describes himself by...'
3. Do not repeat any information.
4. Use your powers of observation to see what is written and what is not written.
5. Do not look at the sample answer until you have tried the exercise!
6. The whole group then constructs a best-shot approach.

When most groups have written an introduction they are again encouraged to read aloud bits of their work.

In terms of competitiveness each group attempt is scored out of 10 by other groups. Further discussion ensues about the skill of writing a good introduction.

The answer below, created by past participants, is not perfect, and it is best if it is critically reviewed. It is thus presented as open for discussion and for comparison with their own efforts.

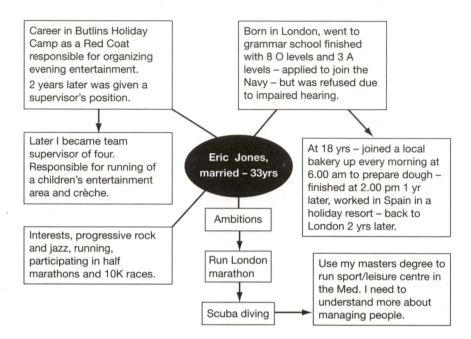

Figure 2.3.1   *Eric Jones: a mature business student studying for an MBA*

Eric Jones has provided a concise summary and overview of his life... with information about himself in the form of a mind map with arrows to direct the reader. The information can be roughly divided into four main topic areas. These cover brief details of his career background, his academic achievements, work experience, his sporting interests and his ambitions... The work ('essay') does not, however, cover his family details or his current employment... He also points to his future aspirations by indicating how his hobbies, past career skills and this new Master's degree will all be used to develop a new business venture...

Finally, in order to increase the degree of reality of the experience, two or three sample introductions could be made available from real company reports, journal articles, previous participants, or from student assignments (eg MBA assignments). These could also be graded or marked out of 10 and the reasons why briefly discussed.

These writing experiences conclude by taking a look at what the textbooks say about writing introductions – comparing participants' own practice with the concepts that are found in writing skills books. The participants can compare what is said about writing introductions using examples from the textbooks.

The following introduction to an interesting essay about popular soap operas is taken from a writing skills book by Peter Redman (2001), called *Good Essay Writing*. It shows how one learner wrote an excellent introduction to a piece of work that looked at *Coronation Street* as a very typical and popular Western soap opera:

> *Coronation Street* consistently gets high viewer ratings. This essay explores the reasons for this popularity, and will evaluate the appeal of *Coronation Street* in comparison with two other major British soap operas: *EastEnders* and *Brookside*. This essay will especially focus on an analysis of *Coronation Street*'s use of very strong female characters, its exploration of women's lives, and its humorous treatment of men. It will contrast these with the 'gritty realism' favoured by *EastEnders* and *Brookside*.
>
> *Good Essay Writing* by Peter Redman, 2001: 46

Participants are asked to develop a checklist of reasons why this has been chosen as an example of a good introduction.

Using the Coffee and papers activity described in Chapter 1.2, photocopies of writing skills texts can be introduced in a quiet and comfortable reading session so that participants can read more about writing good introductions.

After reading and then discussing the reading material they can then be asked to compose a list of the skills required to write good introductions.

From the various writing skills textbooks it is apparent that a good introduction might take the following into account:

- The introduction is the first thing that will be seen by whoever is assessing your essay.
- First impressions are really important and the introduction sets up expectations.
- It should define the main function or purpose of the writing.
- It should indicate the context or historical setting of the writing and include any framework necessary for the reader to understand it.
- It should refer to the style in which the article or report is to be written and explain why.
- It should outline the overall main structure or sections of the article, and its scope, breadth and depth.
- What better way to guarantee a good report than when you tell the reader in your introduction about what the report is going to deliver, and how it is going to conclude?

- It should explain how the different parts of the article interrelate.
- A good introduction will often also say what the report or assignment is *not* going to cover.
- It should highlight what the article or report contains – the main argument or what is new and original – and it sometimes can start debating/defining basic terms.

Part two: the art of writing abstracts, executive summaries and conclusions

This experience is designed to allow learners to develop the skills required to write a good conclusion. This experiential activity uses a real journal article that has had its conclusion removed.

It is important that the paper or journal article is pitched at the right level of complexity, and has general interest and appeal for the audience.

The simple saying below might be introduced as a very simple writing tip at this point:

Three simple steps:

1. Tell the reader what you are going to tell them (the introduction).
2. Tell them – ie the detail or main body of the writing.
3. Then tell them what you have just told them (the conclusion)!

This is of course very crude and unsophisticated reasoning. It is, however, a useful start point for discussion; yet there is more to this skill than this simple aphorism.

Conclusion writing is essentially a 'distillation' exercise – but many writers fail to write a good, concise conclusion that does justice to their work. Why is this so? One of the reasons is that we are often short of time as the deadline approaches, and the conclusion is often the last section to be written. Also, as people reread and edit, they usually start from the front of the work. This process is often repeated several times so that by the time they reach the end of the work, levels of concentration are frequently lower than when starting at the beginning. It is like polishing shoes – some shoes belonging to some people seem to be more often polished at the front but less so the back!

When people set out to write their conclusion they are often tempted to edit along the way and as we see some simple mistakes that we have missed we correct them, instead of concentrating on the job of writing the conclusion. Distractions like this make the conclusion writing hard work. It is best to stay focused on the single task of writing the conclusion.

People rarely give themselves the luxury of focusing specifically on writing a good conclusion. Conclusions are also difficult to write because some people are unsure how to do it, perhaps because no one has ever taught them.

With a long piece of work, the process of remembering the key points that the assignment or essay is trying to make becomes quite difficult. This session is a chance to look at the business of conclusion writing. Sessions can be added on speed reading, as these can aid the process and be beneficial to conclusion writing.

Session instructions

A conclusion should describe the important parts of the whole work, and it must *not* introduce any new information.

Remove the conclusion and the abstract to an appropriate journal article.

One journal paper that has been successfully used several times for this exercise is 'European and Asian telecoms – their role in global sustainable development, by C Beard and R Hartman, published in *European Business Review*, Vol. 11, 1999.

In whatever paper you select, as in the case of the one above, it is best if there are sections that will deliberately distract people so that the ability to focus and concentrate on the job in hand will be tested: the article above, for example, contains numerous charts with a lot of data on fuel consumption and fleet vehicles. This can be regarded as good distracting detail! It is important to make sure that the conclusion has identified the main issues within the article.

Writing conclusions: group instructions

1. You are asked to quickly speed read a journal article.
2. Now reread the article carefully, trying to tease out the main points as you see them.
3. Do this using either of the following:
   - Stick-it labels. Write on them – the advantage is that they can then be moved away from the body of the essay and reorganized. Movement is the key here.
   - Highlighter pens or pencils to make points stand out.
4. Write two or three words maximum in the left-hand margin, saying what each block of text is really focusing on.

5. Now stick all the labels together in a sequence. If using other forms of synthesis such as margin notes or highlighter pens, select the information and rewrite it in a specific order. Using this information as the basic skeleton, expand it so as to form a conclusion for the paper.

6. You are then asked to compare your conclusion by reading one other conclusion that a colleague has written. Compare and contrast and discuss your differing conclusions and make some notes.

7. Now compare your conclusion with the one written in the article that is provided separately.

8. Finally, in pairs make a list of things that you have learned from doing this short exercise.

9. What might you do for your first report/essay/assignment as a result of this exercise?

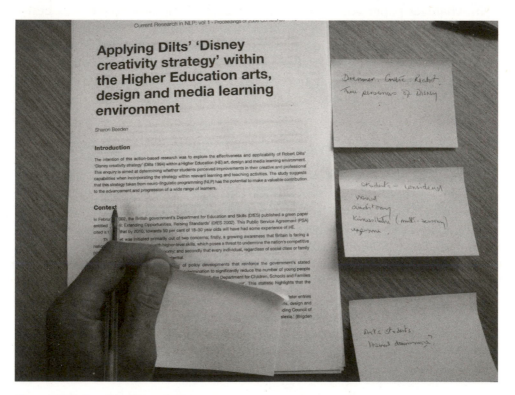

Figure 2.3.2   *Distilling the essence*

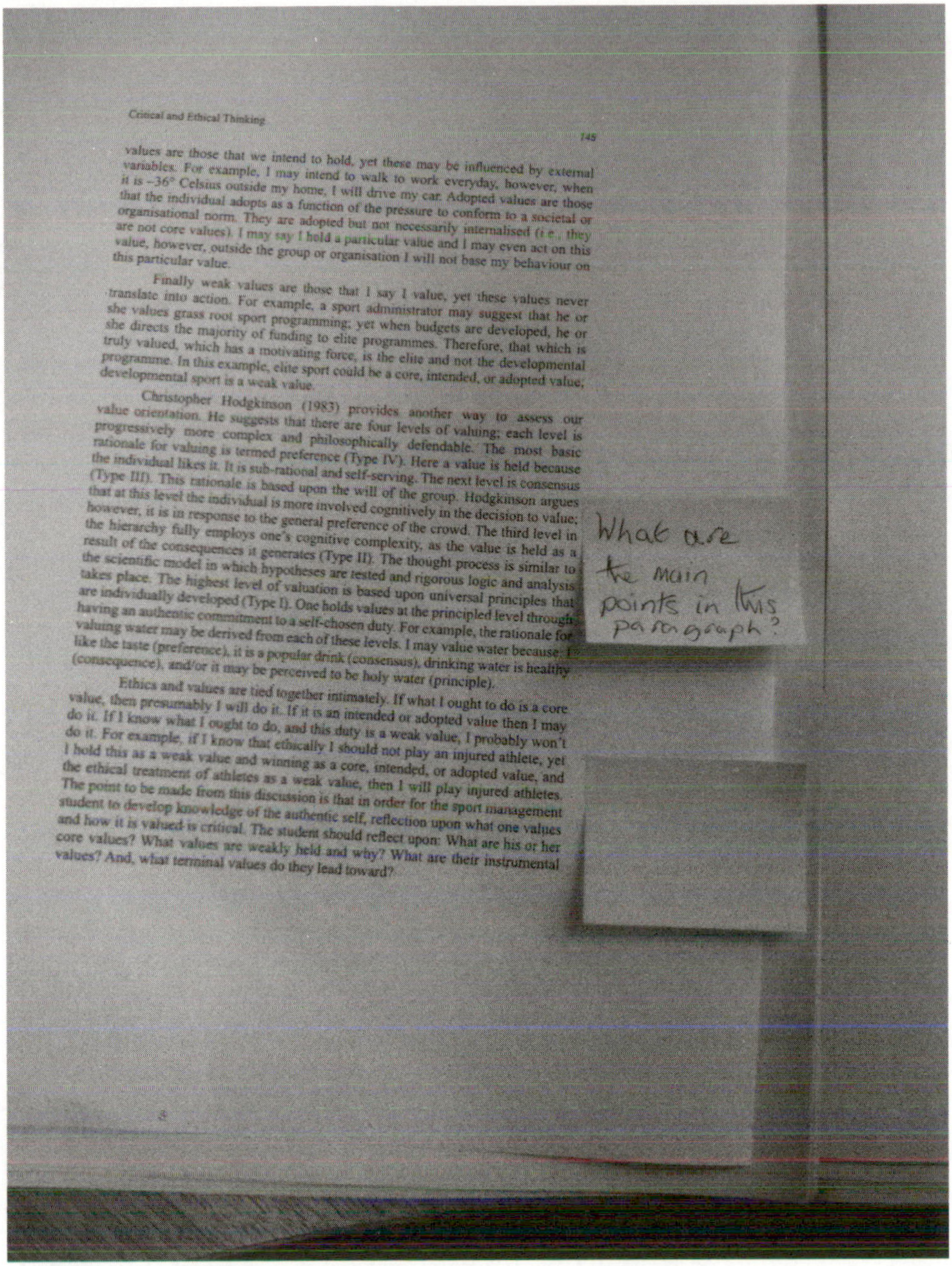

values are those that we intend to hold, yet these may be influenced by external variables. For example, I may intend to walk to work everyday, however, when it is −36° Celsius outside my home, I will drive my car. Adopted values are those that the individual adopts as a function of the pressure to conform to a societal or organisational norm. They are adopted but not necessarily internalised (i.e., they are not core values). I may say I hold a particular value and I may even act on this value, however, outside the group or organisation I will not base my behaviour on this particular value.

Finally weak values are those that I say I value, yet these values never translate into action. For example, a sport administrator may suggest that he or she values grass root sport programming; yet when budgets are developed, he or she directs the majority of funding to elite programmes. Therefore, that which is truly valued, which has a motivating force, is the elite and not the developmental programme. In this example, elite sport could be a core, intended, or adopted value; developmental sport is a weak value.

Christopher Hodgkinson (1983) provides another way to assess our value orientation. He suggests that there are four levels of valuing; each level is progressively more complex and philosophically defendable. The most basic rationale for valuing is termed preference (Type IV). Here a value is held because the individual likes it. It is sub-rational and self-serving. The next level is consensus (Type III). This rationale is based upon the will of the group. Hodgkinson argues that at this level the individual is more involved cognitively in the decision to value; however, it is in response to the general preference of the crowd. The third level in the hierarchy fully employs one's cognitive complexity, as the value is held as a result of the consequences it generates (Type II). The thought process is similar to the scientific model in which hypotheses are tested and rigorous logic and analysis takes place. The highest level of valuation is based upon universal principles that are individually developed (Type I). One holds values at the principled level through having an authentic commitment to a self-chosen duty. For example, the rationale for valuing water may be derived from each of these levels. I may value water because: I like the taste (preference), it is a popular drink (consensus), drinking water is healthy (consequence), and/or it may be perceived to be holy water (principle).

Ethics and values are tied together intimately. If what I ought to do is a core value, then presumably I will do it. If it is an intended or adopted value then I may do it. If I know what I ought to do, and this duty is a weak value, I probably won't do it. For example, if I know that ethically I should not play an injured athlete, yet I hold this as a weak value and winning as a core, intended, or adopted value, and the ethical treatment of athletes as a weak value, then I will play injured athletes. The point to be made from this discussion is that in order for the sport management student to develop knowledge of the authentic self, reflection upon what one values and how it is valued is critical. The student should reflect upon: What are his or her core values? What values are weakly held and why? What are their instrumental values? And, what terminal values do they lead toward?

Figure 2.3.3   *Using highlighters and stick-it labels to identify important themes or facts*

For the article referenced on page 113, highlighted words included:

- **Label 1.** *First para – history/speed of change.*
- **Label 2.** *Service industry, perceived as low environmental impact.*
- **Label 3.** *Research focus = European/Asian companies.*
- **Label 4.** *Huge negative impact. Data – water, fuel, paper, consumption rates.*
- **Label 5.** *Description of 1% phenomenon/GDP.*
- **Label 6.** *Future opportunities.*

It is important that during this experience people realize that sometimes even successful article writers will have to polish and rework their ideas many times. Learners can so easily be led to think that authors can write like this first time. These papers usually take a considerable amount of time to develop.

 ## Resources required

- Plain A4 paper.
- Handout on Eric Jones.
- Study skills books.
- An electronic version of the journal article; or provide your own selection.
- The answer provided above for comparison.

Tip

The minimum time for each of the two main activities is recommended at two hours: one hour for each activity.

 ## References and further reading

Bell, J (1999) *Doing your Research Project: A Guide for First-Time Researchers in Education and Social Science*, 3rd edn, Open University Press, Buckingham

Blaxter, L, Hughes, C and Tight, M (2001) *How to Research*, 2nd edn, Open University Press, Buckingham

Redman, P (2001) *Good Essay Writing – A Social Sciences Guide*, 2nd edn, SAGE Publications, London

Antiques Roadshow: developing product expertise in employees

What it achieves

The experience develops product awareness in groups of people. They can be apprentices or experienced sales staff. In speaking about and handling a variety of selected products, knowledge unfolds through sensing (the touch, feel and sound of products as sensory experiences), careful observation and existing experience.

This fun and adaptable sensory approach generates a deeper commercial knowledge, increases confidence and awareness of company product functions and variable costs about anything from mobile phones to tools and equipment.

Underlying principles

The activity has a practical application for training. It utilizes a concept adapted from the popular TV programme, *Antiques Roadshow*. On this show people bring their own antiques in to be assessed by experts who examine the product while talking about what they see, feel, notice, etc, playing for time to assess the situation while involving the audience in this familiarization process. After a while the exciting subject of monetary value arises at the end of each antique appraisal with the client: 'How much do you think this antique is worth?' The audience waits in anticipation as there are often surprises: the family antique that has been passed down through generations and has simply been gathering dust might just turn out to be worth a lot of money. (However, many turn out to have low monetary value!)

This experience adopts an approach related to morphology, used, for example, in the study of botany or zoology. Morphology is the study of anatomical shape and design in plants and animals and it is a skill that Charles Darwin referred to as the very soul of natural history. The following extract is from a book called *The Kiwi's Egg*, by David Quammen (2007: 193), which takes a fresh look at Darwin's most radical theory:

> What could be more suggestive than that the hand of a human (shaped for grasping), the paw of a mole (shaped for digging), the leg of a horse (shaped for running), the fin of a porpoise (swimming), and the wings of a bat (flying), should all reflect an underlying five-digit pattern, with modified versions of the same bones in the same relative positions? Darwin doesn't claim to be the first naturalist to notice such homology...

These important observations by Charles Darwin were very significant in the development of his famous theory on the origin of species, which permanently transformed our human ideas about life on Earth. With this design knowledge and many years of looking at other forms of life on earth, Darwin was able to provide substantive evidence of the fact that natural selection works upon patterns passed down from ancestral forms.

How to run it

From tools to mobile phones, here we look for patterns, shape, form and possible utility, using simple, down-to-earth powers of observation.

An array of products is placed on a large table or on the floor before or as participants arrive. Each one possesses only a number.

The subject of tools is simply used here to illustrate the technique. All safety considerations should be first assessed – if tools are used, then blades must be covered, etc. A tools catalogue is also placed in the centre of the display of tools. Chairs are placed around the tools and equipment in a circular fashion, one for each of the participants.

Participants are told how the session is going to run and that it is based on a television programme where people take their antiques to a dealer to look at and value – the people on the television often hope that their prized antique will be of very high value – they wait patiently to hear its potential price if it were to be sold!

Each participant is told that volunteering to speak first has a distinct advantage. If there is a simple tool or one that they are familiar with, it will be best to pick it up first and have a go at the task; otherwise they might be left till last with all the most difficult tools remaining – such as a monkey strainer. This can overcome shyness to speak in front of groups.

Each person talks the experience of handling the tool, and in turn each participant picks up one tool, talks through what it looks like, describes its design, what each part might be used for, what the tool as a whole is for, discusses any safety issues, and then comes up with a value for the tool. The person opposite this person is given the tools catalogue with pictures, etc, and while the other person is talking has to find the tool and its price or value. The person describing the tool has to finish with a value, ie what price they think the tool would cost to buy. The facilitator does not interfere with the conversation and only offers encouragement – especially if the participant gets their interpretation or facts right. The facilitator adds more information after the person has finished.

A brief discussion might follow when all the tools have been dealt with. An extensive range of tools can be experienced in this way. This exercise can be used before developing expertise in a bigger, more complex activity such as a fencing project or bridge-building task, and the connection of the tasks with the basic tools can be made.

The approach is learner-centred, involving choice, decision making and active fun engagement in the design of the learning experience. The emotional climate is also addressed. Health and Safety issues and values can be easily embedded into this activity. This activity is particularly good for inexperienced people who are new to this kind of practical assessment work. With commercial products such as mobile phones, for example, it can also be an early part of a sales-training exercise.

Resources required

- Products (tools, phones, beauty products, camcorders, etc).
- Catalogues with current prices and product descriptions, marketing literature, etc.

Tips

This exercise can be adapted for many commercial and non-commercial products. It can also be used for manual work training or health and safety, dentistry equipment and practices, or for fault-finding techniques. This experiential activity has been used in chainsaw courses and tree-felling courses where participants had to identify faults in the chain and guide bar, which then isolated other problems with chain tension and lubrication, etc. This kind of experience has been undertaken with FE college lecturers to develop theoretical concepts for a new foundation-degree course in hair and beauty. A dozen or so lecturers were simply asked to bring three or four hair and beauty products from their handbags and the experience started from this point.

 **Reference**

Quammen, D (2007) *The Kiwi's Egg*, Phoenix Publishing, London

Hearing voices: voice work for reception and call-centre training

What it achieves

Five simple experiences are offered here to improve the voice in, for example, reception and call-centre staff.

Voice transformation is nurtured and developed through this learner-centred approach. A number of small experiential activities are linked together to create multiple voice-work opportunities, so that change occurs gradually.

Underlying principles

The session introduces concepts and sequences of flow. It uses the lowering of levels of reality to begin with, by experiencing or observing and discussing the customer-service skills present in other people as experienced from real life events.

Learners research and then model excellent customer-service scenarios in different formats. There is learner choice in the decision making and active engagement of the learner in the programme design and development.

The experience involves sharing and exploring voice experiences involving customer-service skills. In this collaborative activity everyone, including the tutor, is learning from these experiences, some of which involve live scenarios. It is delivered with a sense of fun and enjoyment.

Learning and change occur in a transparent and enjoyable way, alongside peers. Learners take on responsibility for change.

The activity constructs simple building blocks of experience, moving from simplicity to complexity, using deconstruction and reconstruction of customer-service skills.

How to run it

The five experiences are sequenced as follows:

1. Warm-up: customer service in typical situations: barman, holiday rep, flight check-in, etc.
2. Live phone experiences: listening and voting, and critical analysis.
3. Working on our own voices in groups – developing a new answerphone message.
4. Dealing with difficult situations and difficult customers – simulations.
5. Dealing with difficult situations and difficult customers – learning from practice and the real thing.

Experience 1

For a starter exercise, almost an icebreaker, learners are asked to consider what they like to see in good service from:

- a barman;
- a holiday rep;
- a dentist;
- a doctor;
- supermarket checkout staff.

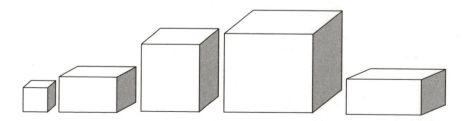

Figure 2.5.1   *Shape, sequence and flow underpin these five small sessions*

A discussion follows as to what has been gleaned from everyday experiences of customer service, as experiential knowing. (A sample handout that could be used as the basis of this session is given at the end of this chapter.)

Experience 2

This second experience is also designed to be fun and act as an icebreaker. Learner views are discussed by the group as a whole. Learners are asked to consider what make of new car they would buy if they were given £15,000.

Ask if any of the group are willing to share their thoughts, to come to the front and describe their new purchase. Give them the imaginary keys and ask them to close their eyes and imagine getting into the car and talk us through it. With men the conversation often goes like this:

> The click of the locking system as I open it, the smell of leather as I sink into the seats... The dashboard is stylish almost like an aircraft, it fits me like a glove and the engine roar seems powerful as I start it up. Then it purrs quietly, waiting...'

Then ask: What does this tell us about customer service and buying goods and services?

The learners are then asked to look in the phone book and find the telephone numbers of four or five car dealerships, hopefully covering some of the models of car they have selected.

The learners are then asked to consider and call out what kind of questions they might ask if they wanted to go and test drive their chosen new car – on Sunday.

The questions to be asked are agreed by the group and might include the following:

- Are you open this Sunday?
- What times are you open?
- For test drives do I need to bring a driving licence?

Using a hands-free phone system and speakers one learner is then asked to ring a car dealership while the other learners listen to the response and score the level of customer care and the voice. Other learners then take it in turns to ring other car dealerships. The responses can be recorded but only used for the learning experience discussion.

The conversations are listened to and the relative merits of each customer-service approach and the voice of the person answering the phone, as representing the persona, is then discussed. Each call is voted on using criteria developed by the learners. These might be tone of voice, sense of interest and energy, care in answering the questions, asking if there is anything else that they can help with, etc. Votes are added up and a discussion ensues.

After allowing time for self-reflection, learners can then consider their own customer-care skills and their own voice abilities – possibly in pairs. Often someone will say, 'I hope I don't sound like that,' or 'I wonder what I sound like.' This is the moment to say, 'Well, let's find out!'

Experience 3

This section involves recording learner voice skills. Learners are asked in pairs to construct and then individually record an answerphone message. There is space to re-record and perfect the recordings. These recordings can then be listened to and discussed in larger groups, depending on the time available. The experience gained about voice from previous experiences is put to use to critically review their own voice work.

Experience 4

People then receive training in dealing with difficult customers, using the four-steps experience in Chapter 1.1.

They are then asked to deal with difficult situations that are role played. These are first talked about, characterized and sketched out by the participants based on their life experiences. They will be familiar with such scenarios.

Working in pairs, people are asked to play the roles of call-centre advisor and a difficult customer. Working towards effective solutions, by continually practising, becomes part of the skills training. The practice involves the development of improved script outlines for certain situations. It is important to show that it is OK to make mistakes and learn to forge good responses together. This creates a 'learning in action, from experience' approach.

Experience 5

People then experience typical work situations, and bring back more real scenarios that can be worked on for further development and honing. The cyclical nature of these experiences thus works towards a positive transfer of learning into real workplace environments and contexts.

Resources required

- Call-centre and hands free phone systems, speakers, etc.
- Voice-recording technology.
- Large whiteboard.

Tips

This session also uses assertiveness skills, and skills for giving feedback and criticism.

This session, with the permission of the learners, can also be used to develop course materials for future learners to use.

Further reading

Carlow, P and Deming, V K (2006) *The Big Book of Customer Service Training*, McGraw-Hill, London

Handout

Fill in the positive and negative experiences you can recall with any three of the following:

- Holiday rep.
- Estate agent.
- Supermarket.
- Barman.
- Hotel reception.
- Dentist.
- Doctor.
- Airport luggage check-in.

Table 2.5.1   *Positive and negative experiences*

Service: ....

Positive experiences	Negative experiences

Part 3

The third dimension: sensing

Introduction

Focus

- Understanding the practical issues of working with the enhancement or reduction of sensory stimulation and the concept of sensory intelligence.
- The important practice question here is: How can the senses be worked with in order to enhance learning?

The more senses we use in an activity, the more memorable the learning experience is likely to be. Optimal sensory stimulation increases the neural connections in our brains and therefore such experiences are made more accessible. Significantly the senses are the means through which the primary information reaches our brains – the senses are the conduits that connect the outer world stimuli with the inner world of our self.

By working with sensory intelligence, the involvement and engagement in a learning experience can be enhanced. Many senses can be stimulated in a learning experience in order to support longer-lasting learning. The five main senses can be stimulated but the body has many other sensors in operation: the body is thus an important site for learning. For all these reasons facilitators and educators should consider the use of the senses to enhance and enrich any learning experience.

The senses can, of course, be overwhelmed by incoming data, and clear benefits can be had by experiencing periods of reflective solitude.

The senses can also be limiting and we can also sense what we want to sense, hear what we want to hear and see what we want to see: here the sensorial experience can be limiting. Some learning activities, of course, deliberately inhibit our senses and awaken others, eg blindfolds are often used in outdoor learning.

The senses form the primary material for us to work with in learning. We internalize this sensory data and make sense of it through the perception of the experience and so move beyond mere assimilation.

Scope of Part 3

Five main activities are presented in Part 3. In order to gain a more complete understanding of the sensing dimension, all five illustrative experiences are briefly explained below.

Experience 3.1: Brand sense

This experience increases awareness about the role of senses in product branding. In addition, this experience is ideal to assist understanding of the role of the senses in learning and development, communication work, facilitator development, training-the-trainer courses, and for educators wanting to use the senses more often in educational work.

Experience 3.2: Blindfold

This experience is a learning activity that illustrates how blindfolds are typically used in outdoor learning. Other sensory approaches are then explored using a range of fun activities that generate a greater understanding of communication.

Experience 3.3: Shape and colour

This experience uses two creative experiences to engage our understanding and discussion of our self. The experience can be used as an icebreaker or to explore learning preferences.

✓ Experience 3.4: The rucksack and the fleece

This experiential approach uses sensory encounters to engage large audiences, demonstrating a learning sequence that first involves telling the audience about something, then showing the audience something of significant interest to the lecture, and then allowing selected people to handle and work with real artefacts to increase levels of engagement and interest. In this case, innovative business products are used to consider design trends and product innovation.

✓ Experience 3.5: Nuts and bolts

This experience encourages the development of skills for observation, classifying, organizing, justifying and defending, and critical analysis.

A range of other concepts to work on in the sensing dimension

1. Ask questions of people: 'What are your senses telling you right now?' Frequently work at this basic questioning level to develop sensory intelligence.
2. Consider how the five or six main sensory modes are stimulated, how they receive information from the external world. Remember there are many other receptors on the inside and outside of the body.
3. The body is a major sensor and is key to impactful learning.
4. The diversity of multiple modes of sensory stimulation increases the diversity of experience and retention of the learning.
5. Our senses can also be limiting if we sense only what we want to sense, hear what we want to hear and see what we want to see.
6. Consider that people do have identifiable sensory preferences as outlined in neuro-linguistic programming (NLP). Sensory preference signals are present in people in, for example, eye movements, language, etc.
7. Consider working with varying forms of sensory enhancement, sensory reduction and sensory deprivation.
8. Use solitude, solo, silence, quiet time, flow and meditative experiences; these are potentially very powerful.

9. Sensory overload or tolerance varies in people and can be problematic.

10. Consider the role of the subconscious in learning, as well as 'presence' and meditative experiences.

11. Walking, talking, reciting and note taking are potentially all forms of sensory enhancement.

12. 'No mind' states generate an emptiness that facilitates the mind as it oscillates between unconscious and conscious.

Brand sense: the role of senses in brand development

What it achieves

This experience increases awareness of the role of the senses in pleasurable experiences. The experience thus focuses on this aspect of product branding.

The experiences are ideal for understanding the role of the senses in communication work, for facilitator development, for training-the-trainer courses, and for educators wanting to use the senses more often in educational work. Learning and development departments rarely create a sense of identity and so brand is a subject opened up amongst educators and trainers.

Underlying principles

Learning occurs through the interaction between the inner and outer worlds. We receive and process information from the outer world through our senses. The human body receives many stimuli, particularly those of taste, smell, hearing, touch and seeing. There are also many other sensory receptors engaging with both the outer world and the inner world of the human body. Many people have preferences about the way they take in information, which appear to be linked to the sensory inputs. For example, some people say, 'I see what you mean,' indicating a preference for the visual. The language used relates to the sensory preferences and this has been extensively studied in neuro-linguistic programming (NLP). This experiential activity is specifically designed to raise awareness of the possibilities for sensory work in experiential learning.

How to run it

In this session people are asked what they would buy if they were given a cheque for £25,000. This exercise can also reveal interesting gender stereotypes; for example, when this experiential activity has been conducted around the world in multinational companies, many men said they would buy a sports car and many women talked about expensive handbags and shoes – but not always!

People are asked to come to the front of the room, close their eyes and tell the rest of the group what it is like to get into their imaginary very expensive sports car, or to have their expensive new handbag. This experience is, of course, a fantasy. People are asked to focus on what it is that actually gives them pleasure. Remarkably, whether the choice is handbags, shoes, sports cars, works of art or books the pleasurable experiences are described in a language rich in sensory description.

Figure 3.1.1   *Sensory language, pleasure and learning*

In a sports car the door opens when they are given the key. The door is solid and as they get into the car they describe the smell of leather as they sink into the seat. The dashboard is also made of leather, and, significantly for some men, it is full of gadgets and instruments: technical wizardry at its best. The engine purrs softly... Likewise, the handbags smell of leather and feel beautiful. One person once described a bag lined with a soft bright pink silk lining... and inside the bag was a beautiful pair of shoes.

This activity then moves on to look at a range of popular products and the sounds, visual images and smells associated with them. This can include Intel and its famous associated sound, Singapore airlines and the branding of the senses, and everyday digital cameras and the noise they make when they are switched on. This is part of the brand, and it is centred on the sensory experience of products.

Participants are asked to fill in the sensory-awareness inventory below, developed by Eric Burns, and to share their personal preferences:

Table 3.1.1 *Sensory awareness inventory (SAI): worked example*

Sight	Sound	Smell	Taste	Touch	Activity
Field in bloom	Good music	Fresh air in the morning	Good food	Touching people	Gardening
Ocean sunset	Waterfall		Good wine	Hug	Hot bath
Beautiful art	Ocean as it hits the rocks	Flowers especially roses	Hot bread	Holding hands	Dinner party
Garden display	Rainfall	Perfume	Roasted chestnuts	Touch of a kiss	Theatre
View from the top of a mountain	The silence of snow falling	Aftershave	Bacon sandwich	Body next to mine	Quiet night at home
Waterfall	High-heeled shoes	Fresh-baked bread	Aniseed	To stroke	Long hot bath
Well-set table	Birds singing	Roasted chestnuts		Hair	Personal shopping
Lit fireplace	Fire	Aromatic herbs		Breeze on my face	Good movie
Morning dew on the grass	People talking in the streets of Italy	Artichokes cooking		Rain on my body	
Animal's body	The sounds of a baby	Newborn baby		Mud on my bare feet	
Rain falling	A room full of people I love			Silk on my skin	
Snow falling	Laughter			A good massage	
People hugging					
A smile					

Ask participants to list under each heading 10–20 items, experiences or activities from which they get pleasure, enjoyment or comfort.

Table 3.1.2   *Sensory awareness inventory (SAI): for completion*

Sight	Sound	Smell	Taste	Touch	Activity

The pleasure of learning

The pleasure of learning is fittingly illustrated by Gergen (1999: 1) in his introduction to social constructionism, where he describes his own pleasures of writing thus:

> I grew up with fountain pens. As a child they were as 'natural' to me as my family. My father's pen seemed to produce an endless stream of mathematical

scribbles that somehow transformed themselves into papers in journals. Meanwhile, my mother's musings gave way to bursts of inspirational writing – short stories, travelogues, and the best letters a boy away from home could ever receive. The pen was destined to become my life. And so it did, as I slowly worked my way toward a professorship in psychology. I loved to ponder and to write; the sound of the pen on paper, the flowing of the ink, the mounting columns of 'my thoughts' – all produced a special thrill…

Furthermore, our senses are alive with memories of the natural. Consalvo (1995: 2) introduced her book of ready-made games for trainers with the following comment, which illustrates the immense sensory richness of the natural environment. Let the imagination flow and recall the sensations:

Blue sky, red sunsets, white puffy clouds, green fields speckled with flowers, pine-covered paths, moonlit meadows, crickets chirping, birds singing, snow crunching under foot, the smell of the spring thaw, summer sweetness, autumn decay, a salty breeze, burning leaves, the squish of mud, the sting of hot sand and the cold of snow are just a few among the plethora of sensory images we experience while outdoors. These sensations often tap emotionally and spiritually uplifting memories.

The senses as the conduits for taking in raw information are often underestimated in terms of their importance in every experience, including learning.

Brand Sense, by Martin Lindstrom (2005), published by Kogan Page, London, shows how to establish a marketing approach that appeals to all the senses, not simply sight and sound. The main argument is that Brands that use two-dimensional strategies of sight and sound should move to a multi-sensory strategy.

Three senses are neglected: smell, taste and touch.

Lindstrom calls for the development of a sensory signature, by doing a sensory audit.

At the end of the book, he gives some examples:

- That gratifying new-car smell that accompanies the purchase of a new car is actually a factory-installed aerosol containing 'new-car aroma'.
- Kellogg's trademarked crunchy sound and feel of eating cornflakes was created in sound labs and patented in the same way that the company owns its recipe and logo.
- Singapore Airlines has patented a scent that is part of every female flight attendant's perfume, as well as being blended into the hot towels served before takeoff, and which generally permeate their entire fleet of airplanes.

The senses we use in communication:

- Sight: 58 per cent;
- Smell: 45 per cent;
- Sound: 41 per cent;
- Taste: 31 per cent;
- Touch: 25 per cent.

Research shows that a full 75 per cent of our emotions are in fact generated by what we smell...

 ## Resources required

- Imagination and courage!
- Shoes and other products for learner choice might be considered.

Tip

Be open to the emergence of sensitive gender issues.

 ## References and further reading

Burns, G (1998) *Nature Guided Therapy: Brief Integrative Strategies for Health and Well-being*, Brunner/Mazel, Philadelphia PA
Consalvo, C (1995) *Outdoor Games for Trainers*, Gower, Aldershot
Gergen, K (1999) *An Invitation to Social Construction*, Sage, London
Lindstrom, M (2005) *Brand Sense*, Kogan Page, London

Blindfold: communication and the senses

What it achieves

Communication is a very broad skill. It involves many smaller skills such as listening, speaking, negotiating, empathy, giving instructions, questioning and presenting. Communication clearly involves more than the face value of the spoken word. Intonation, facial expressions, body movements and other dynamics considerably increase the complexity of human language.

In order to enhance our understanding of the role of our senses in communication, we can work with the senses. Sensory stimulation can be either reduced or enhanced so as to expand the understanding of how they function in learning and in communication.

Underlying principles

This experience initially focuses on visual sensory reduction using blindfolds. Blindfolds are commonly used in outdoor learning activities. The sensory reduction process leads to an increased awareness and the sharpened focus of other sensory modes.

This sensory experience can be used for specific training activities that require sensory reduction or enhancement in order to sensitize people to particular forms of learning. For example, exercises in trust often adopt sensory experiences involving a sighted person leading another blindfolded person.

How to run it

Let us look at five examples using blindfolds:

1. Blindfolded team building a structure such as putting up a tent.
2. Navigating a trail blindfolded.
3. Herding blindfolded sheep by a sighted shepherd!
4. Reducing sight to explore verbal behaviour in groups.
5. Natural blindfolds: caves, listening and speaking for teleconferencing skills.

Putting up a tent is a simple exercise made more difficult by being blindfolded. If one member of the team is not blindfolded, then accurate communication and leadership become an interesting issue. (This is a great exercise for your old tent with a couple of holes in it but you do not want to throw away!) If a tent can be erected while people are blindfolded, then clearly other pieces of equipment might be constructed, and a variety of senses might be enhanced or reduced. Different people could experience different forms of sensory reduction and sensory enhancement. Table 3.2.1 at the end of this chapter lists a range of sensory options.

A blindfold trail can involve, for example, a rope trail, with the rope carefully laid out around trees, over obstacles, under objects, down hills and up hills, etc. As in the tent exercise, all members can be blindfolded or one member can be left fully sighted, or indeed partially sighted with goggles that have had their lenses blurred. A variation on this activity is for team members to solve puzzles or carry out another task while completing the trail: for example, adding up the total age of the whole group, learning first names but in alphabetical order of surnames. Time pressures and/or rules can be added.

The sheep and shepherd exercise requires a team to be the blindfolded sheep and one team member to be the sighted shepherd. Using only a whistle, the shepherd has to round up the sheep, who have been scattered in a field, into an enclosed area. The team can be given a specific amount of time, say five minutes, to develop a whistle code for use in the activity.

In order to explore verbal behaviour in group dynamics, just sitting with blindfolds on and discussing an issue can cause deeper reflection as learners are focusing sharply on verbal dynamics rather than non-verbal behaviours. This can be used to share, for example, performance issues in a team about a previous exercise. Blindfolding can have an interesting effect on the group dynamic and on the ability to listen more carefully and share speaking time ('air time'). Alternatively, two people within the group might volunteer to be blindfolded so that they can listen carefully to the group dynamics and offer feedback at the end of the session. All activities that require people to give feedback should develop basic feedback principles so that they are understood by those required to give it.

An alternative technique here is simply to have a set of coloured and laminated small cards with the following illustrative words printed on them:

- blindfold;
- earplugs;
- fuzzy glasses;
- no talking;
- only listen.

These cards can be used within a group-discussion session and periodically rotated so that different people experience a different understanding of the communication process.

For the natural blindfolds exercise – caves and listening and teleconferencing skills – just sitting in a cave in complete darkness creates a really powerful atmosphere! This exercise can be useful for sensitization about listening and talking. It can be used for teleconferencing skills requiring the ability to share air time, actively involve people or bring them into conversation, and to listen and speak with great care. In Singapore artificial caves have been created out of shipping containers, and some artificial climbing walls now have caves located behind the face of the climbing wall.

 **Resources required**

- Sets of blindfolds (next time you travel on a long plane journey, save the blindfolds!).
- Tents.
- Whistle.
- Rope.
- Caves.

Tips

Besides blindfolds, other sensory stimulation or deprivation techniques can be used – see the sensory checklist below. The senses have an exceptional capacity. The following example from Gladwell (2005: 182) highlights the great potential for using the senses to enhance learning from experience, by allowing subconscious knowledge to be accessed and developed:

> Mayonnaise, for example, is supposed to be evaluated along six dimensions of appearance (colour, colour intensity, chroma, shine, lumpiness, and bubbles), 10 dimensions of texture (adhesiveness to lips, firmness, denseness, and so on), and 14 dimensions of flavour, split among three subgroups – aromatics (eggy, mustardy, and so forth); basic tastes (salty, sour, and sweet); and chemical-feeling factors (burn, pungent, astringent). Each of these factors, in turn, is evaluated on a 15-point scale.

Table 3.2.1   *Working with sensory intelligence in experiential learning*

SOUND	Voice work. Musical and other instruments. Music for relaxation (CDs, etc). Music affects the rate of breathing, blood pressure, pulse rate and muscle activity. Natural sounds, tides, wind, sounds of whales/dolphins, sounds of heartbeat. Human sounds, poetry, lectures as digital voice files, storytelling, humming, mantras. Interview tapes. Whistles, horns and timer alarms, wind, live telephone conversations for customer-care training, tape-recorded instructions for learning activities.
Enhancement	Earphones. Staccato (energetic) powerful voice. Tubes or tins and string to amplify or create distance, microphones, tubes, megaphones.
Reduction	Silence. Ear plugs, distracting sounds. Over playing music. Caves. Reflective meditation. Quiet slow voice. Garden shed. Mountain top. Sleep.
SIGHT	Colours, size, shape and form. Visual language. Light and dark. 3D images. Shadows. Letters, pictures, models and concepts. Maps. Noticeboards, planning documents, art. Masks. Large sheets of paper/glass for information. Stick-it labels.
Enhancement	Big screen, glass screens, binoculars/telescopes, magnifying glasses, mirrors, enhanced lighting, torches, large colour-coded cards, video clips.
Reduction	Object focusing, blindfolds, pillowcases, darkness, caves, darkened rooms, maps with bits missing, incomplete pictures to assemble.
SMELL	Food and drink. Aromas, coffee, fruit, citrus, natural air, fresh air, flowers, perfumes, other plants such as herbs.
Enhancement	Aromatherapy… awareness and appreciation… orange smells in room put near fan of OHP projector.
Reduction	Desensitization. Nose plugs.

TOUCH	Rough, smooth, hot, cold, fingers, skin, feet and toes, surfaces, ground, trees, hairy, smooth, etc, bare earth, soil, water, materials, textures.
Enhancement	Bare feet, sensitize fingers, artificial cave surfaces – eg gravel, stones – ramps, tiles, soft, balls, gooey, string dangling, put hand in box and feel…
Reduction	Gloves, cling film, handcuffs, instructions… not allowing touch – only to look.
TASTE	Food, liquid, acidic, sweet, sour, salty.
Enhancement	Clean palate, quality food, energizing food, refreshing liquids, food therapy… relaxing drinks… natural forest tastes. Orange improves communication, basil and lemon increase mental clarity, pine is refreshing and inspirational, Ylang-ylang relieves anger, bergamot is calming and found in Earl Grey tea.
Reduction	Slowing down food or liquid, reducing energy levels through relaxing food or liquid, taste deprivation, remove certain foods from menu, diet control, cravings.

 # Further reading

Gladwell, M (2005) *Blink*, Little, Brown and Co, New York
Martin, A, Franc, D, Zounkova, D (2004) *Outdoor and Experiential Learning: An Holistic and Creative Approach to Programme Design*, Gower, London

See Bike it! (Chapter 2.1) for more ideas on rule setting, placing of obstacles, and other ways to be creative with simple exercises.

Also refer to the activities involving the use of solar rucksacks to charge phones, fleeces made from plastic bottles, and sensory overload (Chapter 3.4).

Shape and colour: using the senses to generate conversations about learning and personality

What it achieves

This experience is used to generate conversations that enable personal information to be surfaced and shared. These experiences have potential for short icebreakers or for self-awareness through group conversations.

This projective experience gets groups of people to discuss how they see themselves, how they learn and how these facts are connected to personality.

Underlying principles

This activity uses the concept of projecting personal thoughts or ideas onto a shape, colour or object. Particular shapes or colours can reveal some remarkable similarities about, for example, the way people learn or their personality. The choice of shapes is influenced by the left- or right-brain dominance of an individual. This concept is adapted from work on geometric psychology, first developed by Dr Susan Dellinger, who has kindly given permission to refer to her work detailed in *Communicating Beyond our Differences: Introducing the Psycho-Geometrics System* (1996).

This sharing experience is active, and it can be a compelling introductory exercise. In metaphorical terms, John Medina in his book *Brain Rules* (2008) calls these colours, objects (eg Russian dolls) or shapes 'memorable door handles' that access or retrieve personal data located in filing cabinets within the brain.

How to run it

Any four simple shapes such as a triangle, circle, square and a squiggly line can be drawn on four separate flipchart sheets (or large card). One shape is then placed in each of the four corners of a room, so that they can easily be seen by everyone.

A similar experience can be carried out with four primary colours.

People are asked to consider which shape they like the most in the shape example. Time should be allowed for people to have a few moments' thought about their preference.

Each person selects only one shape and they are asked to go and stand in that corner with any other people that like that shape.

Each group then discusses their commonalities and differences as to why they all like that shape. The conversation clearly revolves around a specific shape and discussion usually involves comments such as 'I like the rounded shape because it is very holistic,' 'I like the square because it's very bounded and so you know where you stand. I like to know exactly where I'm going and what I've got to do,' 'The squiggly line has no beginning and no end and I like it. It is creative and free-flowing.'

Allow plenty of time for everyone to talk and air their views.

Each group is then asked to discuss what this information might tell them about 'how they like to learn'. The conversations usually switch effortlessly into understanding the relevance of the shape reference to their learning.

The groups choosing the various shapes differ according to the type of people on the event. Circles tend to be favoured by rounded people, who like the holistic shape. Those preferring squares often have discussions about how they like to know their borders, they like to know what they have to do and they like clear boundaries. Those favouring squiggly lines tend to like artistic creativity, nonconformity, are comfortable with no clear route, no beginning and no end. The discussions can be allowed to be as flexible and creative as participants like. Each shape group then joins with another shape group to listen to other stories, and eventually all four shape groups meet and share. A lot of the focus is on difference and preferences and this makes a good start to any learning event.

This kind of activity can also act as a preliminary investigation into small-group dynamics and group strengths and weaknesses as they work together. Group activities can often be more effective when the groups themselves have a clear understanding and appreciation of their own dynamics, and the characters and personalities involved.

The same approach can be taken for colour, and the discussion can be more personal. Blue, for example, often provokes thoughts about the sky and spiritual feelings, the colour of infinity, of no end, beyond our understanding. Green often evokes comments about the natural and calming. But these discussions can flow in many directions. Different colours can evoke different personal conversations in a group.

red	blue
green	yellow

Figure 3.3.1   *Colour and psychology: icebreaker and learning activity*

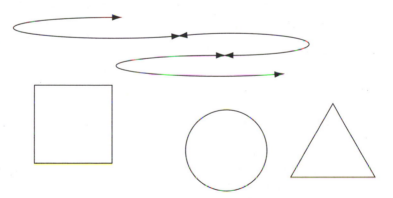

Figure 3.3.2   *Geometry and psychology: icebreaker and learning activity*

Resources required

- Coloured pens.
- Large white cards or flipchart paper.

Tip

Try collecting notes and learning about typical approaches to colour interpretation and shape interpretation, and then try introducing another approach, such as a specific set of objects. Be prepared to experiment.

References and further reading

Dellinger, S (1996) *Communicating Beyond our Differences: Introducing the Psycho-Geometrics System*, Prentice Hall/Jade Inc, Tampa FL; http://www.psychogeometrics.com
Medina, J (2008) *Brain Rules*, Pear Press, Seattle WA
Winston, R (2002) *Human Instinct*, Bantam Books, London

The rucksack and the fleece: effective presentations

What it achieves

This experience activity focuses on using sensory experiences in presentations involving large audiences. This experience also demonstrates how using a sequence of first telling the audience about something, then showing the audience something, and then allowing selected people to handle and work with real artefacts can significantly increase levels of learner engagement and interest.

In the illustrative case described below, innovative business products are used. The focus will be on design trends and sustainable product innovation.

Underlying principles

The activity uses sensory experiences to enhance large-audience participation. Sensory theories suggest that the more the senses are stimulated, the more the learning experience is enhanced. There is also the suggestion that we find it easier to remember things when they are associated with sensory recall. Some senses can be hard to engage with in large-audience interaction, such as in a lecture theatre with some five hundred people in it.

While this theory suggests that touch is of less significance than other senses in learning, this activity uses touch and kinaesthetic experiences – ie receiving information in terms of a physical, bodily experience – in large-audience inter-action and engagement.

This experience also explores the 'Tell, show, do' triangle, a principle developed by Edgar Dale (1969). Dale worked on instructional techniques and suggested that people learn more when they actually do something rather than when simply hearing about it or seeing it. If all three experiences of hearing, seeing and doing are used, then learning is likely to be greater.

How to run it

Dale suggests that the least amount of learning comes from listening and being told, which mostly involve the auditory memory. However, if learners are shown, they will learn more, but not as much as if they were to do a thing or experience it for themselves.

Telling, showing and feeling the fleece

Below are field notes that were taken while working with trainers from AIG Taiwan in 2007. The session involved a large lecture theatre and a number of trainers were exploring ideas for engaging large audiences. The notes that were developed were from reflective observation of video material after the event. The notes reveal how sensory reduction, sensory overload and sensory enhancement can be used to engage large audiences.

> Learners were told about the fact that clothing can now be made from recycled plastic bottles. The level of interest was clearly mediocre. On showing the audience a plastic bottle and some clothing made from the very same plastic the level of interest increased noticeably. However, when the trainer walked among the audience, allowing people to feel the softness of the outdoor fleece jacket, the level of interest and engagement of those selected to feel the material and of the rest of the audience was noticeably higher.
>
> When presented with outdoor clothing material made from plastic bottles as a form of sensory enhancement of the learning experience, the trainers coded this experience as S-e, the 'S' for sensory, the 'e' for enhancement. Feeling the real thing proved to considerably increase learner interest and engagement and the experience of the soft but plastic material is clearly enhanced. A number of people in the lecture theatre were given the material to feel and asked to comment on it to the others in the audience. 'Hmm… it is very soft… remarkable…' they said. After letting several people feel the

fleece, the trainer then rather mischievously moved to let another learner feel the material and then withdraw it as they reached out. The audience laughed at first but then a discussion took place to explore why people had a desire to feel the material, what the impact of withdrawal was and how this highlights the desire (S-d), for an enhanced sensory experience (S-e).

Those who were unable to feel the material remarked that they felt that they had been denied the whole experience. It was a much reduced sensory (S-r) experience. Here there are strong links to the issue of reality (real experiences of the fleece material or the rucksack described below) in learning activity design.

The rucksack

A rucksack, provided by Voltaic Systems at substantial discount, was used to highlight some concepts about business products and sustainable development to a large audience. It is illustratively used here to show how mediating artefacts (real objects/things) can be used as sensory phenomena so as to create greater audience engagement.

The rucksack has solar panels on the back. Inside there is cabling for the charging of phones, iPods, cameras and other technological equipment. Audiences over a number of years have been fascinated by the rucksack. A presenter might first talk about it without allowing participants to see it. Then they show it. It can be taken round the audience so as to let participants touch it and ask questions. The presenter can then demonstrate how to charge a phone using the free power acquired from artificial light in the room. The presenter can then ask someone with low battery power on their phone if it is OK to charge it. The presenter finds the appropriate connection and the phone is charged in front of the audience. Cables running down the straps on the rucksack enable a phone to be charged while on the move, direct from the solar panels.

Interesting intellectual engagement with the audience occurs when the presenter places the rucksack on someone's back and they bend over to collect more energy from the light in the room. The presenter then asks the audience to imagine if a number of people, all wearing solar rucksacks, went into a large, brightly lit supermarket. The presenter asks: 'How much light could we steal without anyone noticing in terms of the fact that it would not have any effect on the supermarket electricity bill?' The audience's level of intellectual engagement steadily increases. These questions unfold and reveal a new way of thinking about energy. Indeed, people begin to wonder how many of us could take this 'free energy'. Where is this energy going if we don't take it? How much energy is available anyway for free consumption? Is it free and who pays for it? Where does it go if we don't use it? Why is the supermarket not utilizing this energy? How much energy is being lost and why not embed voltaic cells into the floor so as to capture and recirculate energy?

Figure 3.4.1   *Rucksack with solar panels*

Developing intellectually challenging questions

Question 1. If a lot of people entered a brightly lit supermarket and charged their batteries, how many people could get free power without affecting the electricity bill of the supermarket? How much light could we therefore recycle in this way?

Question 2. Kinetic watches are not new. Kids have kinetic shoes that light up. If we transfer such technology into the floor in places where thousands of people walk daily, such as a shopping mall, how much power could be generated?

Question 3. One side of Sheffield Business School in the UK frequently has very strong winds blowing down one side. Could deliberate design of high-rise buildings create colossal wind tunnels between them so as to deliberately generate free electricity from wind turbines?

 Resources required

- Real products that have a sustainable development component in their design (they act as mediating artefacts, for audience engagement).
- Instead of real products, large colour images can be used, or film clips.

Tips

Gradually build a set of these resources to show to participants.

These techniques can be good for developing an ideas factory where business product design creativity can be enhanced.

Allow ideas groups to make a pitch for their ideas, with peer score voting and prizes or rewards.

 **References and further reading**

Refer to the *Journal of Sustainable Product Design* for ideas.
Dale, E (1969) *Audiovisual methods in teaching*, Dryden Press, New York

Nuts and bolts: systematic thinking – classifying and organizing

What it achieves

This experience develops systematic thinking, as in time management, job analysis or the creation of filing or storage systems. It involves skills of classifying and sorting, and organizing. Critical analysis occurs through the creation of an opportunity to justify and defend the design systems.

Underlying principles

In these exercises everyday objects act as physical metaphors to develop selected skills and knowledge. The teaching of systems thinking occurs through a detailed analysis of objects. The objects are nuts, bolts, screws and nails. They are presented for subsequent classification, to create and defend the creation of a classification system or typology. These skills of systematic thinking and organizing are required across a range of work and educational disciplines.

How to run it

Learners are divided into small groups and each group receives a bag of various nails, screws, nuts and bolts that are randomly mixed. The groups are informed that they have to develop a classification scheme that systematically separates the items into differing types. Each type must be described in terms of its uniqueness. For example, what is a screw, how many different types of screws are there, and what distinguishes each type? (This is similar to the established rules of the Linnaean system used to classify living creatures.) Learners must be prepared to defend their classification system orally under cross examination.

Groups are encouraged to consider the issues associated with the differences between classifying inanimate objects rather than living organisms. Participants have to present a classification (phylogenetic) chart outlining their scheme, using poster paper, tape, and objects.

The groups are given a list of probing questions that might occur when defending their systematic classification (these can be given on cards, etc to the group), such as:

● What is the rationale used for the development of each category?
● What are the criteria that differentiate each category?
● Did the system rely more on form or function?
● Is there any derivation or lineage?
● Do different types occur in all countries?

An identification key can also be required so that any item of screw, nail, bolt or washer can be picked up and identified using such a key.

Time management

The organizing experience above can also be adapted to time-management skills. The many jobs that people do in their work and non-work lives usually relate to a wider purpose. It is easy to lose sight of this wider purpose when there is much to do.

The everyday jobs are similar to the bag of nuts and bolts and screws and nails. There seems at first sight to be little order.

Order is created when these jobs are linked to a job description. The jobs then have a focus and it is possible to see if the right amount of time is being spent on doing the right things, ie if they contribute to where people want to get to. Efficiency is spending the right amount of time doing things. Effectiveness is spending the right amount of time doing the right things. Efficiency therefore has one 'right' in it, while effectiveness has two 'rights'!

One way to support the understanding of time management is to sort and organize all the jobs into an order. The metaphor of a tree is useful here. The mass of everyday jobs are the leaves. There are many leaves. However, leaves fit onto twigs and larger branches. The branches in turn fit onto a trunk. The trunk is where we want to go in life. One main branch might represent where we want to get to in terms of work, and the other main branch where we want to go with non-work, such as our personal life and family.

The smaller branches are the main areas that we have to achieve – and balance is crucial here. Fitness, health, family commitments are all part of the mass of leaves of everyday life. The filing, sorting of e-mails, maintenance of contacts, writing of reports, the sending of invoices and many other jobs are the leaves of everyday work life.

A list of everyday jobs is created. Then a large tree of life is drawn on a flip-chart. The systematic organization of everyday jobs starts to make sense when they are placed alongside a branch that in turn is attached to a trunk. The contribution of the leaves to main branches is visible. Stress can be reduced when there is some sense of organization and direction.

Resources required

- Bags or boxes.
- Assorted nuts bolts, screws, etc.
- Large sheets of paper – wall-lining paper or flipchart paper.
- Marker pens.
- Rules of classification.

Tips

Allow the learners to create their map on a large sheet of paper and then the classification system can be drawn up and the nuts and bolts removed. Groups or individuals can then compare and contrast their charts with others, and consider other rationales as to why materials were classified in certain ways. This material can be collected by tutors and used to gather different systems and disseminate to groups in future for discussion of the merits of the different systems, etc.

This activity can be specifically applied to the teaching of taxonomy and classification (eg for zoology or botany).

 **Further reading**

This activity is adapted from: http://jrscience.wcp.muohio.edu/lab/taxonomylab. html.

See also Beard, C and Wilson, J (2005) Ingredients for effective experiential learning: the learning combination lock, in *Enhancing Learning in Higher Education*, eds P Hartley, A Woods and M Pill, Kogan Page, London.

Part 4

The fourth dimension: feeling

Introduction

Focus

- Understanding the practical issues of working with the emotions.
- The important practice question here is: How and in what way do the emotions influence learning?

The way we feel about the experience has a strong impact on the effectiveness of learning. While emotional experiences and emotional intelligence underpin learning, many educators and trainers have only recently given more attention to emotional literacy, emotional intelligence and emotional competency.

Waves of emotions are part of our lives; there are emotional 'ups' and 'downs'. Different waves, different sizes and different frequencies all create the essential roller coasters that form the emotional self. Balance is therefore a central theme I wish to encourage. Negative states can be destructive, yet they can also be harnessed as positive. Emotional blocks to learning can include fear and risk aversion as well as the need for perfection and control.

The role of positive emotions in learning seems to be a neglected area: we tend to focus on deficit models. In learning and development we rarely ask ourselves 'What is it that I am enjoying right now?' The positive and negative aspects of emotional engineering are considered here in providing ideas to access the emotional being through the use of projection: onto objects, through metaphor, stories, drama, fantasy, trilogies and emotional mapping.

Emotions work with our social and cognitive self, they are pervasive, interwoven into facets of our inner and outer worlds. They are also linked to the roots of our identity. 'Reframing' emotions helps to alter the inner emotional scripts in our minds, helping us, for example, to the positive potential in negative scenarios. People who show anxiety before giving presentations can reframe their fear. Why do we like to hold our hands up on white-knuckle rides? It appears this is to increase our feelings of fear. So when we make a presentation, maybe it is OK to 'feel the fear', the dry lips, the shaky knees. The experience can be transformed in our mind into a phenomenon to be enjoyed as a thrill.

In this dimension of the learning experience the senses form the basic conduit from the external experience to be translated into an internal stimulation. The stimulation of the senses creates a significant affective response, one that is a powerful determinant of subsequent learning. The senses and the emotions are thus potential gatekeepers to cognitive processing and learning.

Helping people to be conscious of their emotional experience can allow them to better manage and self-support their learning. In this part of the book I share ideas about the ways to read emotional signs, and to work with emotions as part of experiential learning. I offer ways and spaces to access the roots of emotion and ways to surface feelings and challenge emotions. Humour, meta-phors and storytelling can all be used to access and influence the emotional connection to learning and are covered in a more theoretical sense in *Experiential Learning: A Best Practice Handbook for Educators and Trainers* by Colin Beard and John P Wilson (2006).

Helping learners to sense, surface and express both positive and negative feelings rather than deny or censor them requires great skill and care in group work. It enables the colour and richness of the feelings of learners to be expressed and considered in a controlled way so as to maximize learners' understanding of the learning processes.

Scope of Part 4

Five main activities are presented in Part 4. In order to gain a more complete understanding of the feeling dimension, all five illustrative experiences are briefly explained below.

✔ *Experience 4.1: Ace of spades*

This experience uses four representational playing cards to access inner feelings and thoughts. Physical objects are used here to create space to express our feelings: the playing cards are objects used to create different conversations in different spaces, in this illustrative case in the four corners of a room. Individual and collective thoughts about doing, knowing, feelings and change are expressed and explored. Decisive action around a range of generic life options is also encouraged.

Experience 4.2: Accessing emotions

This experience opens up space for discussions and exploration of the feeling dimension of learning through the exploration of word metaphors, visual metaphors and object metaphors.

Experience 4.3: Reframing, rewriting, rethinking

This experience encourages people to address and consider their underlying rationale to the inner voices or scripts that create fears and anxieties.

Experience 4.4: Unfinished statements

This experience can be used for many different types of learning experiences. Unfinished statements are used to provide a variety of emotional spaces to access, express and reflect on feelings about, say, an opinion, a training programme, an outdoor learning event or the experience of a semester of teaching at university.

Experience 4.5: String lines

This experience maps and re-examines emotions related to a journey, be it a life journey, a work journey, a learning programme or a journey through a semester at university. The string and the shape created by it facilitate the surfacing and communication of emotions and feelings.

A range of other concepts to work on in the feeling dimension

1. Do not be afraid to work with and make more transparent the feeling dimension in learning.

2. Ask yourself 'What feelings do I want to engender in my groups or individual students?'

3. Establish your own metaphors for yourself and the learning climate: helper, gardener, sage, travel guide.

4. Emotions can act as the gatekeeper to engagement and cognitive processing and to learning and change.

5. Emotions are inextricably intertwined in the whole life world of learners: their bodies, life projects and relationships.

6. Emotions are experienced as a roller coaster continually moving towards stability and balance.

7. The emotions of learning are especially affected by peers and other significant social relationships.

8. Primary emotions include the opposites of pride–shame, joy–fear, motivation–boredom, anxiety/tension–energy/relaxation.

9. Utilize the concept of emotional 'space' – to surface, express and acknowledge both positive and negative emotions; negative emotions can generate positive feelings when expressed and surfaced.

10. Positive emotions are said to develop resilience and help overcome difficult situations.

11. Make emotions part of the discourse of learning – transparent and OK.

Ace of spades: space for reflection

What it achieves

This experience is a group-reflection activity. It not only explores what people have done and what they know, but also how they feel and what action they might take in the future. These different elements of reflection occur in different physical spaces.

Underlying principles

This experience is selected to focus on the ways to encourage individual and group conversations about feelings. Physical objects, in this case four playing cards, are used to facilitate thoughts and feelings.

How to run it

This reviewing and reflection experience is based on an idea by Roger Greenaway (see www.reviewing.co.uk). Learners are asked to develop four differing reflective expressions of an event or events.

Each reflective expression occurs in a different corner of a room. Each corner represents a different conversation, and the varying voices of what was done, what people felt, etc are separated into different spaces. Learners move on from each space when they have finished talking about each reflective element. The four elements are:

● Diamonds = facts: the doing dimension;
● Spades = findings: the knowing dimension;
● Hearts = feelings: the feeling dimension;
● Clubs = future: the changing dimension.

The ace of diamonds is in the first corner and represents 'hard' facts, as diamonds are hard. Here in this corner there are discussions only about doing, what we did or I did. Only the hard facts can be reviewed in this first corner of the room.

People then move to the next corner, where the ace of spades is waiting. The spade is for digging and here people dig below the surface of doing, and ask 'What is it that we now know that we did not know before this experience?' This is the findings element.

People then move to another corner of the room, where the ace of hearts awaits them. This card represents the feelings element, and questions might include 'What did we feel about today or that particular event when...'

The ace of clubs is waiting in the last corner, representing the three life options: 1) leave it as it is; 2) remove the situation or people altogether; or 3) alter or change the situation or person in a positive way. In this part, the future, we must ask ourselves 'What are we going to do about this? What do I do next?'

Learners can proceed in large or small groups.

This session can be very effective after the first day of a training event as it allows for participants to have space to talk without the tutor, and the tutors can be called in at the end of the exercise so that participants can tell them what they would like to happen next.

Another variation is to place all the cards on the floor or table and let people pick up a card and then talk about the appropriate category.

Resources required

● String and stick-it labels.
● A pack of playing cards.

Tip

The website www.reviewing.co.uk is full of information and links to other sites, including an amazing array of helpful information developed by Roger Greenaway, who specializes in reviewing skills, evaluation and facilitation. Over 100 reviewing activities can be found here.

Accessing emotions: popular metaphors

What it achieves

The following experiences use metaphors to open up space to explore the feeling dimension of learning.

The activity looks at visual metaphors, word and phrase metaphors and object metaphors.

Underlying principles

Metaphors enable us to see – they can help learners get a picture, an idea, a word or a phrase. Metaphors can also limit us to one view.

Metaphors can lower the sense of reality when dealing with the feeling dimension and so can present less personal threat to our persona when we talk about them.

Metaphors can open up a space for the exploration of feelings, often with comparative ease.

How to run it

Michael Gass in 1995 produced a book about metaphors for use in outdoor learning. Metaphors, he said, present a powerful tool to access and explore feelings:

A single word can possess multiple meanings; yet as the common saying goes, one picture can be worth a thousand words. And if one picture can be worth a thousand words, then one experience can be worth a thousand pictures. And if an experience can be worth a thousand pictures, then one metaphor can be worth a thousand experiences. But in the end, a metaphor only possesses value when:

● it is able to interpret the experience
● in a manner that provides a picture
● that produces words
● that have meaning
● for that particular person.

In 1993 a popular book about communication between men and women hit the headlines. It was called *Men are from Mars, Women are from Venus* (Gray, 1993). On the back of this book the promotional piece said:

Once upon a time Martians and Venusians met, fell in love, and had happy relationships together because they respected and accepted their differences. Then they came to Earth and amnesia set in: they forgot they were from different planets. Using this metaphor to illustrate the commonly occurring conflicts between men and women, Dr John Gray explains how these differences can come between the sexes and prohibit mutually fulfilling loving relationships.

A metaphor can provide another way of reflecting and focusing on a particular experience, so allowing us to gain new insights. A metaphor is a figure of speech that transfers meaning.

The word itself is derived from the Greek *meta* (trans) and *pherein* (to carry).

Word metaphors

Mortiboys uses the following metaphors in his book, *Teaching with Emotional Intelligence* (2005: 17):

● law enforcer to the potentially criminal;
● carer to the vulnerable;
● advocates to the jury;
● salesperson to potential buyers;
● preacher to the sinful;

- sheepdog to sheep;
- website to surface;
- guru to followers;
- gardener to plants;
- tour guide to the occupants of a tour bus.

He then asks the reader to choose which of these metaphors is the best fit most of the time for them as a teacher.

Morgan in *Images of Organizations* (1997) stated that 'the use of metaphor implies a way of thinking and a way of seeing that pervade how we understand our world generally'; and perhaps more significantly he said that 'all theory is metaphor'. Through his research, Morgan identified a number of metaphors that allow us to think about issues of work in organizations from a variety of perspectives. Each metaphor provides insights and also constrains our ways of thinking. The types of metaphors Morgan identified were:

- the organization as a machine;
- the organization as an organism;
- the organization as a brain;
- the organization as a culture;
- the political organization;
- the organization as a psychic prison;
- the organization as a flux and transformation;
- the organization as an instrument of domination.

People share and critically discuss these metaphors in the following ways:

- what the metaphors mean to them;
- why they do or do not see themselves using them;
- what best and worst bits could be taken away from this range of metaphors.

If these are not suitable, people may want to create their own metaphors.

The chosen metaphor will of course have an underlying attitude and disposition associated with it. Mortiboys asks people to consider the underlying feelings that are triggered by any metaphorical adoption and what is triggered in the people you work with.

Visual metaphors

We can also work with visual metaphors. One that I often use in focus groups is a picture of a tree. People are variously portrayed on this image. Some are trying to climb up the tree, some swinging from a rope and some are stood at the base of the trunk, looking puzzled. Other people are climbing further up the tree. Two people are sitting halfway up the tree, with their arms around each other, admiring and savouring the view from the branch. Further up, people are reaching the dizzy heights near the top, and one person has success-fully conquered this giant tree and stands proud with their arms in the air and a big smile: they have made it to the top.

For students in higher education or people looking at their careers, this becomes an interesting visual metaphor. I ask people to consider what the picture says to them. The responses are always interesting.

Some people feel they are only just starting out, while others are progressing well up through the tree. Others notice that they may not be finding time to savour the view, smell the roses and enjoy their new friendships, as they are in a bit of a rush to get to the top. Some people remark that this leads to a rush to get to their idealized place: for university students some note that they seem to be rushing to get a degree, to get their ideal job, ideal salary and ideal children, house and car. And they say with some amazement that maybe what they are doing is deferring life because of this almost obsessive rush to get on, to do and get in order to become happy later.

Object metaphors

The same process can be used with leaves, stones or any artefacts people may want to bring. People are asked to discuss these objects and why they like them and what they mean to them.

Russian dolls can also be used as metaphors to represent size (power) and distance (reporting to or closeness to others), for discussion of workplace issues.

Figure 4.2.1   *A visual metaphor (source unknown)*

 Resources required

- A list of metaphors.
- Metaphors can be placed on cards for learners to choose and discuss.
- Visual images if necessary.
- A range of objects if needed.

 Tips

Allow plenty of space for this activity, in order to explore sensitive issues.

Gender issues might use the metaphor of men being from Mars, women from Venus.

People might bring along a book title as a metaphor for discussion.

Work metaphors can be gleaned from Morgan (1997), and these can open up interesting lines of discussion.

 References and further reading

Accessing emotions through popular metaphors is covered in *Experiential Learning: A Best Practice Handbook for Educators and Trainers* by Colin Beard and John P Wilson (Kogan Page, 2006) (pages 206–11).

Gass, M (1995) *The Book of Metaphors, Volume 11*, Kendall/Hunt Publishing, Dubuque, IA, USA

Gray, J (1993) *Men Are from Mars, Women Are from Venus*, Thorsons, London

Morgan, G (1997) *Images of Organizations*, Sage, London

Mortiboys, A (2005) *Teaching with Emotional Intelligence*, Routledge, London

Reframing, rewriting, rethinking: the emotions of fear and risk

What it achieves

This experience encourages people to address, reconsider or confront the underlying rationale that creates personal fears and anxieties.

Underlying principles

Personal fears can be debilitating in many subtle ways. They can also be based on irrational thought processes.

Fear and anxiety in relation to learning from life can be addressed through the processes of reframing and rewriting the inner voices in our heads. These irrational scripts can be changed by working with the feeling dimension of learning.

How to run it

Emotions influence everyday behaviour, and they can have a distorting effect on learning. Interestingly, anger and aggression are often based on fear, and trust is a strong antidote to fear. Fear is one of the strongest primary emotions, which can be both conducive to improved learning and toxic to learning. Fear is the result of powerful emotional circuitry embedded in the brain resulting in a conditioned response. Mallinger and De Wyze (1993) describe these fears as being present in many people, and they describe people who pride themselves on being reliable, hard-working and self-disciplined; they are indeed regarded as perfectionists. Their offices and homes are neat and organized, and they are always in control. They are successful and financially secure. The downside is that while they may be confident and poised on the outside, they may be hurting inside, for their standards are so high they constantly set themselves up for disappointment, and such perfection may prevent them from enjoying life and even forming relationships. Being too much in control can result in being out of control. Such fears need managing so as to create balance. Learners with signs of being 'too perfect' might have:

● a fear of making errors;
● a fear of making the wrong decision or choice;
● a strong devotion to work;
● a need for order and a firm routine;
● emotional guardedness;
● a tendency to be stubborn or oppositional;
● a heightened sensitivity to being pressured or controlled by others;
● a need to know and follow the rules;
● an inclination to worry, ruminate or doubt;
● a need to be above criticism – moral, professional or personal;
● a chronic inner pressure to use every minute productively.

Adapted from Mallinger and De Wyze, 1993

Rewriting the script of the inner voice

In order to help people address fear using less dramatic methods than some activities that require a confrontation using physical activities, here the experience consists of asking people to spring-clean their own self-imposed 'inner rules' that sit in their unconscious mind. Learners can rewrite their own rules and realize that it is OK and human to make mistakes. Learners can learn to value themselves, warts and all, loosening the grip of perfectionism. There are three basic steps that can prove helpful; on a sheet of paper they should write:

1. The script of the inner voice (in the left-hand column):
    – I must never show my nerves in public.

2. Which really means (in the right-hand column):
    – I couldn't stand the embarrassment if people saw me looking flushed and nervous.
3. So we revise the rule:
    – I prefer not to show my nervous feelings in public... but if I do, people will understand. Importantly, it would not be the end of the world. Most people feel nervous about these things at one time or another. I might not like it but I can cope with it.

Working in pairs, people are then asked to rewrite the scripts suggested by Mallinger and De Wyze:

● I have a fear of making errors.
● I have a fear of making the wrong decision or choice.
● I have a strong devotion to work.
● I have a need for order and a firm routine.
● I have an emotional guardedness.
● I have a tendency to be stubborn or oppositional.
● I have a heightened sensitivity to being pressured or controlled by others.
● I have a need to know and follow the rules.
● I have an inclination to worry, ruminate or doubt.
● I have a need to be above criticism – moral, professional or personal.
● I have a chronic inner pressure to use every minute productively.

Reframing

In this experience people are asked to look at positive possibilities in everyday seemingly negative events. Let me give some examples.

There is the famous Chinese story of the man who lost his horse. All his fellow-villagers came to say how sorry they were about his loss. But the man simply said, 'We'll see.' The horse, however, returned with other horses from the wild and the man then had more horses than before. Then his son broke his leg; again the villagers came to say how sorry they were to hear the bad news. The man simply said, 'We'll see.' Then the army came to take the young people away to war. But the man's son was not conscripted, because of his broken leg. And so the story continues...

A personal story from my own experience involves arriving for an interview on the Scilly Isles many years ago – on the wrong day. It all went completely wrong. In hindsight such an idyllic job on the Scillies with a cottage thrown in was actually not the right move at the time anyway. As it turned out, there were other things that provided more fruitful life experiences. The interview as a story to friends also generates a funny aspect to the experience. This interview could have been interpreted, of course, as a rather tragic life event, a big mistake.

People are asked to choose two things that currently and/or consistently produce negative thoughts or emotions. After showing or telling the above stories as examples, people work on reframing their negative thoughts or emotions.

By rewriting a new script, consisting of good possibilities and reasoning rather than bad news, a new vista may be opened up, especially when shared and discussed with other people.

Paradoxically, people on roller coaster rides hold their arms in the air to increase the pleasure of fear!

 ## Resources required

- Examples of reframing.
- Lists of irrational fears.

 ## Reference

Mallinger, A and De Wyze, J (1993) *Too Perfect*, HarperCollins, London

Unfinished statements: sentences that access the feeling dimension

What it achieves

This session can be used for many areas of learning, but here it is used to work with the feeling dimension by opening up emotional space to access and reflect upon personal and group feelings and emotions.

Underlying principles

A simple loose-leaf booklet is developed with selected statements that when answered encourage and allow space for feelings and emotions to be expressed more easily than they would if people were just asked to discuss them.

How to run it

Develop a booklet of unfinished statements. These might include:

- The most enjoyable part of the outdoor week was during...
- For me the funniest moment was when...
- The event that caused most anxiety for me this semester was...

- I liked working with you when...
- My greatest fear was...
- I felt confused about the...
- My best moment of pride occurred when...
- I felt a bit guilty when...
- I was angry when...
- The most boring bits were...
- I was sad when...
- What I really like about working with you is...
- My own lack of confidence is usually caused by...
- I easily get upset when...
- It doesn't seem right when...
- I am happiest when I am...
- What I like about reading is...
- For me the best bits about work are when...

The statements can be used to variously explore a range of feelings, covering, for example:

- friendship;
- peacefulness;
- anger;
- fun;
- anxiety;
- boredom;
- confusion;
- enjoyment;
- envy;
- fear;
- frustration;
- inadequateness;
- pride;
- sadness.

Furthermore, depending on the context of the learning and development, the statements can cover:

- personal life;
- work life;
- adventures;
- holidays;
- partners.

Learners can work alone and in private, or they can choose someone they want to work with as a pair. People are briefed as to the protocol for speaking and listening. The booklet is designed so that one person speaks and the other listens, so that the unfinished statements are answered by alternating them between two people. Taking turns allows listening and speaking to be rotated. Learners find a quiet space to be comfortable and relatively alone; this can be indoors or outdoors.

The booklet usually has an introductory page to be read out by one reader, and then it is simply passed back and forth, taking turns to read out and then finish a statement. Each statement might or might not warrant more discussion. It is best if the unfinished statements are not followed slavishly in quick sequence, ie with short answers; it is best when relaxed discussion takes place on each response.

Alternatively, the statements can be written answers rather than spoken. And again they can be completed alone or in pairs.

 ## Resources required

Laminated statements cards for more permanent use and use in the outdoors.

 ## Tips

The booklet can be laminated and holes punched in the top corner; in this way booklets can be reconstructed in different ways and new questions created.

An alternative activity is to ask people to finish off ten lines of:

I am...'

These are then explored to look at what has been declared and these are then classified into physical, roles and identity, emotional, mental, etc.

 ## Further reading

See the chapter on working with emotions in *Experiential Learning: A Best Practice Handbook for Educators and Trainers* by Colin Beard and John P Wilson (Kogan Page, 2006).

String lines:
exploring journeys in life

What it achieves

This exercise creates space for the expression of positive and negative emotions about life journeys, including family journeys, work journeys or study journeys. The experience explores emotional balance.

Underlying principles

Physical objects, in this case string, can be used to allow projection of thoughts and feelings. String allows the surfacing, mapping, examination and communication to others of positive and negative emotions about a variety of life journeys. The string is particularly useful in that its length represents time; the string can be as long as is required to reflect upon a specific life journey.

How to run it

Long lengths of string and packs of stick-it labels are given to people. They are then asked to find a space to be alone. Ideally a floor or table space is required. People then create up-and-down shapes with the string. The ups represent positive emotional periods and the downs represent negative periods. These can relate to specified themes, such as the training programme, the last year at work or university, or family life, the experience today, life so far, etc.

The waves are then annotated with information on stick-it labels so that the significant positive and negative events can be identified and talked about with others. The life-journey information might also variously enquire about the extent to which the stories relate to dimensions of being, doing, getting, knowing and changing in relation to the positive or negative feelings.

After allowing time for self-reflection, learners can then find another person to share their waves with and listen to each other's stories.

Life mapping

People can be asked to review their whole life to date on a piece of string: one end represents birth, the other end represents death. Significantly a knot has to be tied at the current age and the string is shaped to create waves up to the knot. People will often talk about the high emotions associated with getting their first job, getting married, having their first baby, getting their degree or promotion.

A more detailed reflective analysis might reveal the extent to which these things are associated with getting, doing, feelings, as in identity roles such as architect, father, or physical achievements such as winning a medal in a race.

The straight line after the knot often has an impact on people in that they feel that they might indeed be able to influence what they do with the remainder of their lives.

A professor in human resource development that I know writes down 10 goals each year. These are goals that he wants to achieve to create balance in four main areas of his life:

● his mind;
● his body;
● his emotions;
● his spirit.

To ensure a consistent focus each day he sets specific 'SPICE' goals: spiritual, physical, intellectual, career and emotional. These help him either to stay on course or to change direction.

The waves in the life map again represent emotional highs and lows in life. Interpreting and sharing these can be a powerful experience, and the idea of creating a future can be either uplifting or emotionally daunting. With this in mind I often refer to Desmond Morris (1969: 158), who suggests that the object of any life journey is a struggle and this takes the form of a desire to experience 'optimum stimulation'. However, he adds:

When a man is reaching retirement age he often dreams of sitting quietly in the sun. By relaxing and 'taking it easy' he hopes to stretch out an enjoyable old age. If he manages to fulfil his 'sun-sit' dream, one thing is certain: he will not lengthen his life, he will shorten it. The reason is simple – he will give up the 'Stimulus Struggle'.

While this 'struggle' for balance in life, for optimum experience, is for the most part an emotional one, it can take on many dimensions. The struggle is in doing things, getting things, sensing things, feeling things, knowing things, being oneself and becoming someone.

Finally, here is a reminder of some life principles that are worthy of consideration:

- If people live with criticism, they learn to condemn.
- If people live with hostility, they learn to fight.
- If people live with ridicule, they learn to be shy.
- If people live with shame, they learn to feel guilt.
- If people live with tolerance, they learn to be patient.
- If people live with encouragement, they learn confidence.
- If people live with praise, they learn to appreciate.
- If people live with fairness, they learn justice.
- If people live with security, they learn to have faith.
- If people live with approval, they learn to like themselves.
- If people live with acceptance and friendship, they learn to find love in the world.

Resources required

- Long lengths of flexible (not stiff) string.
- Stick-it labels.
- Pens.

Reference

Morris, D (1969) *The Human Zoo*, Corgi Books, London

Part 5

The fifth dimension: knowing

Introduction

Focus

- Understanding the practical issues of working with the way the mind processes learning.
- The important practice question here is: What are the cognitive processes at work in learning?

Everyone has a different intelligence profile.

Ways of knowing

In this section I seek to explore the differing ways of knowing. The way in which information is seen, organized and processed is central to knowing and thinking. Edward Cell, in *Learning to Learn from Experience* (1984), suggests that we 'need to reformulate [information], draw consequences from it and use it in other ways to solve problems'. Two lenses through which we can view knowledge are explored in the practical experiences below: they are vertical interpretations (higher and lower) and horizontal interpretations (breadth). These views enable learners to see the connectivity and continuous oscillation between simplicity and complexity. The practical experiences explore the movement and connectedness between types of knowing, including bodily knowing, experiential knowing, practical knowing and propositional knowing.

We have explored cognitive processing in relation to different spaces and to the importance of bodily movement. The movement of the information itself is increasingly recognized as important for certain kinds of cognitive processing. Getting information is not so problematic these days, as the internet has made access relatively easy. There exists a contemporary shift away from the simple transmission of information by educators and trainers towards the transformation of knowledge and knowing.

The brain has two hemispheres. They are responsible for different cognitive functions. The left hemisphere is responsible for logic, numbers, concepts and language. The right side of the brain is responsible for non-verbal, visual and intuitive work. This hemisphere is also responsible for imagination. The right side of the brain likes to be given an overview.

Processing and organizing skills are essential cognitive functions that develop sound, higher-order thinking. Cell (1984: 196–7)) outlines three organizing skills and five processing skills:

Organizing skills:

- Structure: understanding by classifying, defining, and making and applying rules.
- Relation: understanding by relating one thing, idea or experience to another.
- Comparison: understanding by comparing or contrasting one thing, idea or experience with another.

Processing skills:

- Analysis: breaking a whole down into its unique parts.
- Synthesis: combining separate elements to form a coherent whole.
- Convergence: using a number of facts or clues to solve a problem.
- Divergence: creating a variety of alternatives for action or interpretation.
- Deduction: seeing implications; reasoning from premises to necessary conclusions.

Intelligence

Earlier ways of testing intelligence were controversial and used questionable approaches. Here 'types' of intelligences are considered in order to understand the more acceptable argument that people possess different intelligence profiles. In the previous section, emotions were explored. The concept of 'emotional intelligence' (EQ) was initially developed from the work of Howard Gardner, and it was Gardner's book, *Frames of Mind* (1983), that proposed several forms of intelligence, including: linguistic; logical, mathematical, scientific; visual, spatial; musical; bodily, physical, kinaesthetic; interpersonal; and intra-personal. He maintained that there were other forms of intelligence and stated that: 'We should spend less time ranking children and more time in helping them to identify their natural competencies and gifts and cultivate those. There are hundreds and hundreds of ways to succeed, and many, many different abilities that will help you get there' (Gardner, 1983). Therefore, in learning, the recognition of and the ability to work with individual intelligence profiles are important.

Gardner's multiple intelligence (MI) theory can be summarized as follows:

1. Linguistic intelligence = word smart;
2. Logical/mathematical/scientific intelligence = number smart;
3. Visual/spatial intelligence = spatially smart;
4. Musical intelligence/rhythms = sound smart;
5. Bodily/physical/kinaesthetic intelligence = body smart;
6. Interpersonal/social feedback skills/peer work = people smart;
7. Intra-personal intelligence = self smart;
8. Emotional intelligence = emotionally smart;
9. Naturalistic intelligence, awareness of environment, wildlife, etc = nature smart;
10. Spiritual intelligence = life smart.

Wisdom

There is, of course, intelligence beyond these descriptions, such as intuition and wisdom. Wisdom is briefly explored in Listening to silence in Chapter 1.5. Egan in *The Skilled Helper* (2002: 19) talks about a 'common-sense wisdom' found, for example, in the helping professions. Egan suggests that helpers, including educators and trainers, 'need to be wise, and part of their job is to impart some of their wisdom, however indirectly'.

Wisdom finds itself when the voice of the ego is silenced, and the experience of life develops self-knowledge that matures thinking and understanding. Wisdom creates a mind that refuses to let experience become a liability through the creation of blind spots. Egan reflects upon some interesting defining statements about wisdom, such as:

an expertise in the conduct and meaning of life... an expert knowledge system concerning the fundamental pragmatics of life.

Scope of Part 5

Five main activities are presented in Part 5. In order to gain a more complete understanding of the knowing dimension, all five illustrative experiences are briefly explained below.

✓ ### *Experience 5.1: The marketplace*

This experience relates to the development of thinking beyond what is directly observed. The initial interpretation of products is built on so as to develop innovative and creative minds. Using observation techniques, The marketplace experience shows the emergence and further development of thinking patterns. The experience explores basic linear patterns through an examination of products. Cross-product developments and the notion of 'functionality merging' and higher levels of thinking are also explored. Future projections are made through an 'ideas factory'.

✓ ### *Experience 5.2: How to get to...*

The experience commences with everyday knowledge and, through inter-action, creates higher levels of learning through vertical and lateral mapping techniques. This experiential session starts with a simple brainstorming process that identifies potential methods for travelling to work or college in the morning. The answers become the ground layer, the initial building blocks, that ultimately become the complex concepts that represent higher levels of thinking. The technique shows how to move through these vertical and lateral layers.

✓ ### *Experience 5.3: The Singapore obelisk*

This logical/mathematical experience highlights how a simple structure, in this case an obelisk, can be broken down into smaller components for the learners to build. In this case the structure is deconstructed into building blocks and information is given about rate of progress of building, when people do not work and how much building occurs on any one day. For the learners the answer to the problem is to discover when the structure was completed. Thus this exercise applies MI theories by selecting and testing logical/mathematical intelligence rather than being, say, a physical exercise such as the raft-building exercise often used in outdoor learning.

Experience 5.4: Skills for researching and consulting

This experience explores the introduction of basic research skills. Consulting styles and research methodology are introduced, using a popular metaphor of 'research as a form of investigation'. Investigation and problem solving lie at the heart of this exploration of knowing.

Experience 5.5: Walk the talk

This experience is suitable for learning across a range of complex subjects. The experience links the roles of mind, body and space. The kinaesthetic or bodily learning embeds potentially complex information more deeply in the memory through a spatial-relational awareness. Learners map and walk the learning while talking aloud. Learners also research material, construct a lineage, map the facts, interpret events in different and critical ways, act as consumers and producers of learning materials, and walk and talk aloud to relate their own interpretations of historical events.

A range of other concepts to work on in the knowing dimension

1. Higher forms of cognitive processing and learning often involve different ways of seeing the whole: through mind mapping both horizontally and vertically (H–V mapping).

2. Self-actualization and wisdom are said to be 'higher' forms of learning.

3. There are a number of different forms of knowing: experiential knowing, propositional knowing, tacit knowing, practical knowing (skill as knowledge and often located in bodily knowing).

4. Higher and deeper levels of learning require space to see, read and process information differently.

5. MI self-profiling can prove interesting for learners in that it increases awareness of the different forms of so-called 'intelligence'.

6. Thinking skills can be taught and developed.

7. Processing experiences more often than not involve altering existing mental schema.

8. Levels of challenge and support can be altered in learning, to learner advantage.

9. Relaxation, peak experiences, playfulness and flow are significant states of mind for learning.

10. Naturalistic intelligence and spiritual intelligence are less well known, and harder to understand, describe and work with.

 References

Cell, E (1984) *Learning to Learn from Experience*, State University of New York Press, Albany

Egan, G (2002) *The Skilled Helper: A problem-management and opportunity-development approach to helping*, Brooks/Cole Publishing, Pacific Grove CA

Gardner, H (1983) *Frames of Mind*, Basic Books, New York

The marketplace: developing creativity and innovation

What it achieves

This experience involves the development of mind patterns for innovation. It is included in the knowing dimension as it involves an appreciation of innovative thought patterns. These patterns of thought are developed by experientially exploring real products, as currently found in the marketplace (present or past).

Underlying principles

This activity focuses on innovation and creativity training. The experience uses observation techniques that develop patterns of thought. These might include linear patterns occurring in products, as seen through a chronological evolution of a product over time. Sometimes product innovation makes a significant leap from one set of functions to a completely different set.

Other patterns are sought, such as cross-product developments where patterns of product innovation initially develop independently but then merge to form a multi-functional product.

An example of a complex cluster of functions is that of a mobile phone with a built-in camera, SMS message service, internet capability, voice recorder, music store, etc. Another example is the rucksack with solar panels built into it.

The activity develops higher levels of thinking, and a prompt list of thinking types is used to aid the process.

How to run it

The session uses real products available in the marketplace. These products are set out in a random manner on a market-stall style of layout across several tables, and participants handle and experience the range of goods. Photographs can also be used. One set of products can be used by the tutor to illustratively explain and show basic trends. Discussion is encouraged concerning the nature of product innovation trends.

The participants then move, sort and order the products in any particular way so that they can illustrate any potential trends they can observe.

This session encourages kinaesthetic experiences, sensory experiences and discussion and interaction to embed the learning (touching, handling, testing out, winding up radios, powering mobile phones and iPods from a solar-panel rucksack, feeling soft clothing fabrics made from plastic bottles).

Figure 5.1.1   *Washing-up brushes, toothbrushes and razors: reducing disposable materials*

Discussion might include corporate social responsibility and environmental impact at product level in the case of the products included in the list of resources below.

Learners wander around, look at products, talk about them, wonder what they are in some cases. Some products are labelled with laminated cards. After 10–15 minutes participants are then encouraged to work in groups to explore the market developments as a whole. Moving the products around, organizing them and building up the higher layers of thinking are important in the development of creative thinking.

Mobility and flexibility of people, information and artefacts are an important aspect of this experience.

Review questions might include:

- What trends can be observed?
- To what extent are the products designed for disposability or longevity?
- Are the products potentially or actually multi-functional?
- What is the separation of disposability and longevity? (Is there a separation of the part that is designed for longevity? See toothbrush, razor, and washing-up brush examples below.)
- Do products get lighter, smaller and cheaper over time as new versions are introduced?
- What linear or cross-product trends can be identified? (Examples are mobile phone developments or cross-product ideas: the laptop bag plus solar technology that result in a solar rucksack; clothes with solar threads that produce 'solar-intelligent' clothing.)
- Can the creative developments be attributed to art, technology, waste-disposal or other categories?
- Can you predict any future design ideas/potential?

A toothbrush has been developed with a removable and replaceable head, thus reducing the disposable element of the product. This is an important consideration for product design in countries where landfill costs are rising and producer responsibility laws are driving down waste production. This separation of the disposable element from the part that is designed for longevity has of course been applied to razors for many years. This separation is also beginning to appear in other handled products such as washing-up brushes.

The session can generate considerable discussion about consumer behaviour and business product design in general. The potential for commercial products to make a positive contribution to the improvement of the planet is a very real challenge to business and becomes a lively discussion point.

At the end of the session an ideas factory can be set up, allowing students to work together to design and invent new products, and develop ideas. Elements of competition through voting and prizes can be included, perhaps using a critical review of innovation factors agreed by participants. A discussion about the potential of future commercial products to create a positive impact on the Earth is central to this session.

The session can also be used in conjunction with the technique called Coffee and papers, with individual quiet reading and follow-on group discussion about innovation and creativity.

The following thinking skills repertoire is taken from work by Edward Cell in *Learning to Learn from Experience* (1984). This list can act as a useful aide memoire to consider the different types of thinking skills:

- Look for structures: understanding by classifying, defining, and making and applying rules.
- Establish relation: understanding by relating one thing, idea or experience to another.
- Comparison: understanding by comparing or contrasting one thing, idea or experience with another.

These are organizing skills. Next are skills concerning processing:

- Analysis: breaking the whole down into its unique parts.
- Synthesis: combining separate elements to form a coherent whole.
- Convergence: utilizing a number of facts or clues to solve a problem. This is reasoning inductively.
- Diversions: creating a variety of alternatives for action or interpretation.
- Deduction: seeing implications; reasoning from premises to necessary conclusions.

✂ Resources required

Photographs or real products can be used. Photographs can be laminated for this exercise.

Tips

Ask learners to bring any of their own items. Learners spend the week before the session monitoring their household waste and noting down everything that is thrown away.

Examples from innovation factory ideas include:

- a multi-functional handle for razor and toothbrush;
- a toothbrush that is battery powered by kinetic energy of hand movement;
- floors with voltaic cells built into them to recycle light energy;
- mats designed to collect kinetic energy, installed in the entrances to large shopping malls.

 **References and further reading**

Beard, C M and Hartmann, R (1999) Eco-innovation: rethinking future business products and services, in *Greener Marketing*, eds M Charter and J Polonsky, Greenleaf Publishing, Sheffield

Cell, E (1984) *Learning to Learn from Experience*, State University of New York Press, Albany

How to get to…:
developing higher thinking

What it achieves

How to get to… develops higher-order processing skills. It develops an understanding of higher levels of conceptual and critical thinking through the experience of organizing and processing information. These skills are important for strategic thinking by senior managers in the workplace and are particularly useful for those engaged in higher education.

These skills are identified in the higher cognitive layers of Bloom's taxonomy of learning domains. These include synthesis, judgement, evaluation, critical, conceptual and creative analysis. The session uses an experientially engaging activity that generates positive learner participation and fun.

Underlying principles

This session starts with a simple problem or statement being positioned in the centre of a large whiteboard. In the future we may be using huge areas of glass screen to do such work.

The handout included with this activity highlights various layers of learning and follows a basic taxonomy. These educational taxonomic levels are the basic principle for the vertical mapping process, moving through from basic understanding, knowing and describing to synthesis evaluation and judgement as shown below.

- Advanced
  - Evaluation: judge, select, recognize, criticize.

- Synthesis: summarize, argue, relate, organize, generalize, conclude.
- Analysis: select, compare, differentiate, contrast, break down.
- Application: predict, select, assess, find, show, use, construct, compute.
- Comprehension: identify, illustrate, represent, formulate, explain, contrast.

● Basic
- Knowledge: write, state, recall, recognize, select, reproduce, measure.

Bass, B S (1956) *Taxonomy of Education:*
The Classification of Educational Goals, Longman, London

Using an engaging title such as 'How to get to work or university: a critical analysis' the session gradually moves learners from simplicity to complexity, and learners experience how to become more critical, conceptual and analytical (for example, in higher-education institutions or university degree-level work).

The technique uses horizontal mapping first, then applies vertical mapping. Obvious spatial connections are made between the lower and higher layers. While horizontal mapping is well known, such as through work by Tony Buzan, vertical mapping to develop higher cognitive thinking is less commonly applied. The approach deliberately generates a sense of fun and enjoyment, especially in the first brainstorming stage, which generates creative ideas.

The capacity of the brain to conduct these higher thinking activities can be limited by the small space used to convey information. A book page or computer screen is limited and so turning over pages affects the ability to see the whole picture. For this reason this activity requires a large area of writing space such as a large whiteboard. Tables or floor space can suffice if there is no large writing space. Cards can also be used instead of writing the answers on a whiteboard.

How to run it

In the centre of a large whiteboard, write the fictitious, fun assignment that is to be addressed: eg 'Student methods of transportation: a critical analysis of getting to lectures in the morning'.

People are asked to call out any means of transport they can think of: tram, car, coach, train, walk, horse, etc.

As these are called out, write them on the whiteboard. Discussion is not needed at this brainstorming stage but often funny comments add to the challenge. If someone shouts out 'Helicopter', for example, you might say, 'We have some wealthy people in the audience!'

Any empty space on the whiteboard seems to encourage students to try to fill it – with more, and often increasingly innovative and interesting, ideas: parachute, skateboard, through the sewers, virtual/teleconferencing, by canoe.

Figure 5.2.1   *Cycling is just one method of getting to college, university or work*

Note: some students may say, 'Qualifications' and virtual ways to get to college. These are interesting and innovative thinking patterns. 'Qualifications' suggests that the learner has interpreted the question in a different way. This is good and they could be invited to explain to the others how they have interpreted the question.

'Virtual' suggests a creative thought pattern (the opposite of real ways to get to college). Encourage these ideas.

This first level of brainstorming represents the hard ground-level work, the building blocks. By this I mean that in reality, in order to answer any assignment question, learners need to go to the library, carry out extensive reading and make a lot of notes – about trams, bikes, parachutes, etc. This is what this stage of thinking is all about and would be full of notes if done by an individual. This represents getting to know the subject or breadth of 'territory' at this first level. The topic or territory is thus mapped out horizontally first.

All these responses represent the first level of thinking – stage 1 as shown in Figure 5.2.2. This figure can be copied and issued as a handout before or after the exercise to show the key words that can apply to each level of learning and highlight the levels of thinking skill involved.

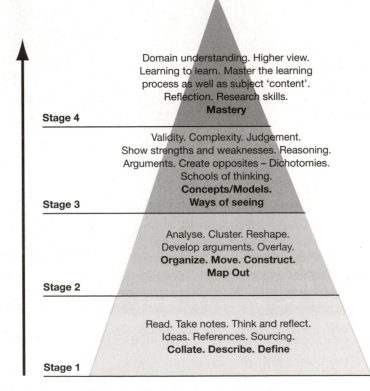

Figure 5.2.2   *A simplified model of the levels of thinking*

Now take a different-coloured pen and ask the students to organize and cluster information from this first level. Figure 5.3 can be copied as a handout and given out to highlight the levels of thinking skill involved. 'Cluster and organize' can be found, for example, in stage 2.

Motorized, non-motorized, human powered, animal powered, by air, by land, by sea, by two wheels, by multiple wheels, slow, fast, etc – these may be the kinds of ideas that emerge at this stage.

Students tend to come up with many ways of classifying stage 1. This builds into stage 2 of thinking.

Next take another colour of pen and construct all the simple opposites from stage 2 and write them down in a list:

- Analysis:
    - motorized–non-motorized;
    - human–animal;
    - fast–slow;
    - public–private;
    - one wheeled–two wheeled, etc;
    - expensive–cheap;
    - real–virtual;
    - single mode–multiple mode;
    - air–land;
    - regular/convenient–infrequent;
    - ground–underground;
    - rail–track–road;
    - mass transport–individual.

This highlights the development of simple constructs. These ideas might then be clustered into 'utility' (speed, cost, convenience, etc), 'location' (air, water, land, underground) and 'propulsion' (human, animal, natural, fossil fuels, etc).

Learners are then encouraged to develop more complex constructs by adding a number of these simple ideas: for example, by creating two axes – building a quadrant model. An example would be to ask learners to consider efficacy, the most 'effective' way for a student to get to university. This often results in agreement that cost and speed are two important utility factors. Cheap transport is fine but if it is very slow it might not be the best way. Cheap and fast might be the best combination. A helicopter is fast and expensive. The participants can then reclassify examples of specific forms of transport types into these new categories.

Table 5.2.1   *A simple construct of utility*

SLOW AND EXPENSIVE eg taxi in rush hour	FAST AND EXPENSIVE eg airplane, helicopter
SLOW AND CHEAP eg walking	FAST AND CHEAP eg bus, tram

The shaded area in Table 5.2.1 identifies the most appropriate way for the majority of students. A third conceptual dimension might be the extent of environmental damage or carbon impact of the selected methods of getting into college or university.

This involves the generation and justification/evaluation of multiple modelling factors – for example, speed, cost, availability, pollution (personal choice, perhaps). The thinking is now moving to multi-dimensional conceptual thinking or modelling. These are thus more complex constructs.

Environmentally friendly transport might itself be a mixture of several factors. Discussion of such factors can then be included as part of the development of critical analysis.

This critical, creative and conceptual work represents the third level of thinking – stage 3 in Figure 5.2.2.

If students can cope with this, then move on to stage 4. Now you might look at their ability to learn to move up and down the stages – for assignments or problem solving.

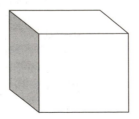

Figure 5.2.3   *Moving on to a three-dimensional framework*

Stage 4 is about mastery and learning to learn. This level is associated with the ability to move up and down the cognitive (thinking) levels. Moving through them is part of good assignment work – but the higher levels cannot easily be reached unless the first level, stage 1, is completed, as this is the foundation layer, representing the hard work of extensive reading and note taking. The list below can be used to discuss the more comprehensive levels and range of skills needed to reach the higher levels of thinking and analysis. It can be copied and issued to participants as another handout.

Skills essential in the development of higher levels of critical thinking:

1. gathering information and utilizing resources;
2. developing flexibility in form and style;
3. asking high-quality questions;
4. weighing evidence before drawing conclusions;
5. utilizing metaphors and models;
6. conceptualizing strategies (mind mapping, pros-and-cons lists, outlines, etc);
7. dealing productively with ambiguity, differences and novelty;
8. creating possibilities and probabilities (brainstorming, formulas, surveys, cause and effect);
9. debate and discussion skills;
10. identifying mistakes, discrepancies and illogic;
11. examining alternative approaches (shifting frame of reference, thinking out of the box, etc);
12. hypothesis-testing strategies;
13. developing objectivity;
14. generalization and pattern detection (identifying and organizing information, translating information, cross-over applications);
15. sequencing events.

Taken from *Brain-based Learning:*
The New Science of Teaching and Training by Eric Jensen (2000)

 **Resources required**

- Large whiteboard.
- Coloured pens.
- Handouts optional.

 Tip

One of the main skills of higher levels of thinking is to see shape and form, trends and patterns and different clusters of information and data. The brain can be trained to do this processing.

References and further reading

Bass, B S (1956) *Taxonomy of Education: The Classification of Educational Goals*, Longman, London

Cell, E (1984) *Learning to Learn from Experience*, State University Press, New York

Jensen, E (2000) *Brain-based Learning: The New Science of Teaching and Training*, The Brain Store, San Diego CA

The Singapore obelisk: multiple intelligence (logical/mathematical)

What it achieves

This task exposes and develops logical/mathematical skills. The experience uses low levels of reality for the participants and has a high level of cultural neutrality. Information sharing, group behaviour and team dynamics are all potentially interesting observational elements.

Underlying principles

Multiple intelligence theory suggests that there are many forms of intelligence. People have differing profiles of intelligence: some have higher levels of being word smart, number smart, spatially smart, bodily smart, people smart or self-smart, for example. This experience demonstrates 'doing' using logical/mathematical problem-solving activities. Other forms of doing can easily be applied to such an activity. Many examples of such logical activities can be found in everyday puzzle books on sale in newsagent shops.

This specific experiential activity involves breaking down a physical structure into many smaller bits of information, including labour involvement and size of the building, etc. This generates salient information. Irrelevant information can be generated in order to be discarded, such as the colour of the clothes the builders are wearing. The learner has to use all the information to reconstruct the structure. This is the basis of the Singapore obelisk (an obelisk is a tapering stone pillar of square or rectangular cross section, set up as a monument).

A theory, a poem, a bike, any structure can be deconstructed or broken down into its constituent parts for the learner to then rebuild.

These kinds of activity can be used for classical teamwork exercises, leadership exploration and communication. The design should not be driven by the task: the trainer or educator should primarily also deconstruct the purpose or observational focus (teamwork or communication, for example). These process issues have to be broken down so that clear learning objectives can be formed.

This particular exercise, using as it does a logical/mathematical type of approach, will result in some learners (possibly those with higher levels of logical/mathematical intelligence – see Part 5 Introduction on multiple intelligence theory) engaging strongly with this kind of exercise while others do not.

How to run it

The facilitator distributes the group instruction sheet (see below), one copy to each member of the team. The information cards are divided up randomly among the team members. The team has to complete the task. The facilitator then leads a review of the experience using the review sheet and, if necessary, the answer and rationale sheet.

Approximately 25 minutes are required to complete the activity, with additional time for review.

Ideally teams should comprise five to eight participants.

Group instruction sheet

On the adventure island of Pulau Ubin near Singapore, a rectangular stone obelisk, known now as the Sing Obelisk, was erected many years ago. Your task is to read all about the details of the building process. Miraculously the structure took less than two weeks to complete and your task is to determine on which day of the week it was completed.

You may share the information you have on the cards but you may not show your cards to other participants.

Notes on variations

Individuals may complete review sheets (see below) individually before the group process takes place.

Extra irrelevant information may be introduced to complicate the task.

Process observers may be used.

Review sheet

- What actions helped the group to accomplish the task?
- Which actions hindered the group in completing the task?
- Who participated the most?
- Who participated the least?
- What feelings did you experience as the task progressed?
- What suggestions would you make to improve team performance?

Did any leadership issues emerge in the team?

Answer and rationale

- The dimensions of the Sing mean that it contains 50,000 cubic feet of material.
- Blocks are 1 cubic foot each, therefore 50,000 blocks are required.
- There are 7 working schlibs in a day.
- Each worker lays 150 blocks per schlib, therefore each worker lays 1,050 blocks per day.
- There are 8 workers per day, meaning that 8,400 blocks are laid per working day.
- The 50,000th block is therefore laid on the sixth working day.
- As work does not take place on daydoldrum, the sixth working day is neptiminus.

Information cards

These can be laminated.

There should be a different colour per group and the cards should be numbered on the reverse to avoid complications if teams lose cards or sets need checking (this point is based on experience!).

Cards can measure as little as two inches by three inches for easy travel/storage.

Place cards and other instruction sheets, etc in a suitable container to look smart; video cassette boxes will do, or ideally something smaller.

The cards should contain the following information:

1. The basic measurement of time in Ubin is a day.
2. An Ubinian day is divided into schlibs and ponks.
3. The length of the Sing is 50 feet.
4. The height of the Sing is 100 feet.
5. The depth of the Sing is 10 feet.
6. The Sing is built of stone blocks.
7. Each block is 1 cubic foot.
8. Day 1 in the Ubinian week is called aquaday.
9. Day 2 in the Ubinian week is called neptiminus.
10. Day 3 in the Ubinian week is called sharkday.
11. Day 4 in the Ubinian week is called mermaidday.
12. Day 5 in the Ubinian week is called daydoldrum.
13. There are 5 days in an Ubinian week.
14. The working day has 9 schlibs.
15. Each worker takes rest periods during the working day totalling 16 ponks.
16. There are 8 ponks in a schlib.
17. Workers each lay 150 blocks per schlib.
18. At any time when work is taking place, there is a gang of 9 people on site.
19. One member of each gang has religious duties and does not lay blocks.
20. No work takes place on daydoldrum.
21. What is a cubit?

22. A cubit is a cube, all sides of which measure 1 megalithic yard.

23. There are 3.5 feet in a megalithic yard.

24. Does work take place on a Sunday?

25. What is a Sing?

26. The Sing is made of green blocks.

27. Green has special religious significance on mermaidday.

28. Each gang includes two women.

29. Work starts on the first day of the Ubinian week.

30. Only one gang is working on the construction of the Sing.

Resources required

- Group instruction sheets.
- Information cards.
- Answer and rationale sheet.
- Review sheets.

Tips

Any type of structure can be used. The format for this type of deconstruction activity can easily be seen. It can also be applied to models or theories.

See also Bike it! in Chapter 2.1.

Digital cameras can be used to take a series of pictures showing group behaviours, which can then be given to the group for self-analysis.

Acknowledgement

This exercise was developed for Outward Bound Singapore, located on the beautiful island of Pulau Ubin near Singapore. It was deliberately adapted to show the process of deconstruction to their outdoor instructors and its original format can be found in the Zin obelisk exercise in *Fifty Activities for Self-development*, by Dave Francis and Mike Woodcock (1982, Gower, Aldershot).

Skills for researching and consulting: practitioner-researcher training

What it achieves

This activity introduces the subject of research, particularly focusing on understanding the teaching of research, research methodology and the importance of literature reviewing, using the concept of research as a form of investigation. These techniques can be useful for organizations like the NHS, for teachers, trainers and for research departments in organizations wanting to encourage and develop practitioner-researchers.

Underlying principles

The experiences described here start from simple concepts and the everyday world of the beginner researcher. Then they gradually take people into the less-known aspects of research, with its increased cognitive complexity and dimensions of reality.

The research process is thus deconstructed and simplified. The complex language and terminology often found in research-method texts is very gradually introduced so as to increase confidence. This language of research is explored and demystified, and jargon is explained.

The journey of learning involves significant collaborative work, and anxieties about research are demystified and addressed through sharing, fun approaches and encouragement of a climate of questioning, fun and collaboration. Active engagement is a significant part of the experience.

Blaxter *et al* (1996) argue that the key skills needed for research, such as listening, reading, watching, selecting, questioning, writing, presenting and organizing, are in fact skills used all the time in everyday life.

How to run it

Methodology is more than just a description of the chosen method(s); this area should embrace the broader questions about what can be known and how it might be known, as well as outlining the selected and deselected methods. Thus it is about taking initially a more strategic view of the investigative approach to the research problem as well as exploring the logic behind the methods selected and not selected.

The initial session applies three main stages to this experience of learning, taking learners through 1) consulting models; 2) exploring how different detection methods work; and 3) traditional approaches to research.

Consulting

Students are given photocopied pages on styles of consulting (Margerison, 1988: 103–113) to read. Each group is allocated a specific consulting style from the doctor, travel agent, detective and salesperson approaches. Each group is then asked to extract key words from their allocated style that best describe the approach.

Each group is provided with a set of wipe-clean plastic cards and OHP transparency pens on which to write (this is a more environmentally friendly approach as the cards can be reused), but it can be done with squares of paper and stick-it labels. The list, containing no more than 10 key words, is then placed in a line on the large table without the style being named. People are asked to identify the four styles from the descriptions alone. For example:

The medical analogy: a doctor style of consulting might have the following characteristics:

● Client-centred/organizational illness to be cured. Searching for good/ normal health, exploring the part of the organization that is ill, unhealthy or unfit for purpose.

● Symptoms/diagnosis/medicine to be prescribed: operation – cut out the unhealthy bit.

People explore and discuss the differences and similarities across the styles. Having examined the four consulting styles, people are then asked to discuss their own preference for a consulting style or styles, giving their reasoning. Often people say they prefer the travel agent style as it is strongly client-centred and very neutral in providing a service based on asking questions and providing choices, thus offering options according to need and cost and other requirements.

The use of the detective style is then explored in more detail. One of the consulting styles is that of a detective or 'investigator'. The experience then moves on to look at different famous fictional detectives. Here people examine the idea that research is also a form of investigation.

Detecting

When doing a research dissertation people are in effect investigators. In taking a closer look at the detective style of consulting, and after discussion, people often conclude that in research this consulting style descriptor of apportioning blame is less appropriate in research, although we may draw other similarities with research, for example how important it is to collect important information, possibly as evidence. There are many other similarities that are also discussed.

The experience then moves on to look at five very different detective characters and their differing approaches. These are known in the popular media and they were drawn on in a detailed journal article about research by Thorpe and Moscarola in 1991. In this article five detectives are described:

- Hercule Poirot;
- Sherlock Holmes;
- Maigret;
- Columbo;
- Dirty Harry.

People are given the Thorpe and Moscarola article to read and divided into five groups and allocated one detective, with no group knowing which detective the other groups have been given. As before with consulting styles, key words are extracted and placed on different-coloured sets of cards, without the name of their detective, with all the groups eventually attempting to identify the different characters from the words alone.

In one particular session of this exercise, the group also watched some brief film clips of these fictional detectives to bring the thinking alive as an experience. Interestingly, we learnt that the character of Sherlock Holmes was created by a doctor, Sir Arthur Conan Doyle, who wrote the Holmes books while waiting for his patients to arrive, and who admitted that his skills of deduction had been gleaned from his medical professor at university.

People work out which key words go with which detective, and look for chains of association within each row. Because different-coloured cards have been used, it is very easy to see the emergent links and patterns within each particular style, then draw out the similarities and differences across the five approaches.

This selection and identification process introduces new researchers to basic research skills. Some of the key words that emerge and are associated with specific detectives may be:

- science and microscopes (eg Sherlock Holmes);
- proven facts;
- listening and trying to understand;
- prodding and pushing (Dirty Harry);
- being intuitive;
- unconventional;
- deductive reasoning;
- chemical testing;
- facial observations (Hercule Poirot);
- logic.

People very quickly recognize that, with care, the range of words and phrases can be related to a range of academic research activities. This can stimulate discussion about the various ways or methods to go about collecting 'evidence', information or data. During this discussion, we can introduce the notion of deductive and inductive reasoning, thus making links between data collection and analysis.

People also pick up very quickly that the values and culture of both detectives and researchers will be influenced by a range of factors, which will in turn influence their theoretical and methodological approaches. If trained in the natural sciences, then the approach is very different. How reliable are facts? What is a 'fact' anyway? What is truth? People now begin to recognize the emerging questions that they have created through the experience so far. Reflexivity and their own influence and impact on research are acknowledged as significant to the research process. Gill and Johnson (1991) maintain:

> It is important to realize that the prior experiences, values and theories of the researcher will determine how one goes about researching and thus determines what you 'see' and do not see... there is perhaps no independent or neutral point from which an investigator might occupy and objectively

observe the world and thus all knowledge is knowledge from particular points of view or paradigms.

Gill and Johnson, 1991

People may remark that all these detectives are men. This issue of gender and feminist research approaches can then be discussed and additional reading material provided. This allows the portrayed characteristics of fictional women detectives to be discussed. For example:

- Jane Tennyson;
- Hetty Wainthrop;
- Miss Marple;
- Dr Kay Scarpetta.

In the session of this exercise referred to above, we then moved on to look at two very different pieces of research. Two fictitious and very different dissertations were presented. The first had a research question that looked at the effect of height on work performance in high-rise offices in cities such as London or Singapore. The second piece of research looked at the myths and legends associated with training and development programmes.

People were divided into two groups for this next experience. Working on a large table, two research titles were written on large cards and placed at either end of a long strip of masking tape, thus presenting a dichotomy. A brief for each dissertation was also provided on the reverse of the card. The high-buildings research was to be done mainly through existing company documentation and the research design was to attempt to 'prove' a hypothesis that height above sea level did not affect work performance within buildings. The other topic was in principle an inductive approach, using stories from the field as raw data, with the researcher having no strong preconceived hypothesis for testing; rather, they wanted to let the data unfold and expose further interesting research questions. Underlying the research, however, was a desire to uncover and surface some of the hidden beliefs, myths and folklore associated with training programmes. The research sought to investigate these phenomena through stories from people that had attended training courses.

A range of identical research words, as shown in Table 5.2, was given to each of the two groups. (These were in fact put in old video boxes with a cover designed with pictures of detectives.) People were then asked to place the words along the masking-tape line connecting the two topics. If the words suited one research approach, then they were to place them near that end. If unsure, they might place the words in the centre of the masking-tape line. If the words were not understood, they were left out and explored with the use of a glossary of research terms found in texts such as Gill and Johnson (1991). The two groups compared responses through discussion either during or at the end of this part of the experience.

This experience generated considerable discussion and the onset of some frustration since some word responses could not be clearly demarcated as belonging to one research approach or the other. People recognized that in general they were working with quantitative and qualitative, inductive and deductive, topics and that some concepts fell clearly into one area or the other, although, as one student said, 'But I might want to find out whether people felt that height affected their performance, and surely that is qualitative?' This squared the circle beautifully with our earlier discussion on the influence of researcher interpretation on the process.

At this stage the notion arose that the research approach is dictated both by the subject or topic and the desires, preferences, background, training and experiences of the researcher.

A third topic can then be introduced and more cards presented (see below). This then dispels the idea of a simple dichotomy and so creates a more complex research mosaic:

Why do mature women return to education? Getting to the truth?

Table 5.4.1   *An introduction to research language*

High buildings	Myths and legends
objective, observed from a distance	inductive
material, matter, things, objects	working with social beings who create meaning and who constantly make sense of their world
scientific, natural sciences	
control and effect	no group values are wrong
stimulus and response	powerful everyday stories used by ordinary people – common sense is valid
logical, deductive approach	
to discover neutral laws so people can predict and control events	ethnographic
	subjective
hard facts	qualitative
positivist, verifiable, measured, demonstrated	to understand and describe meaningful social action
statistical analysis, computer analysis	
quantitative	interpretive social science

This subject was the focus of a PhD and has been written up as a book and so is available to use in this experience (Parr, 2000). People often suggest the answer might lie in the idea that women return to 'get qualified' later in life and start a career. The doctoral research into this question is then discussed and the underlying notion of women 'regaining their sense of identity' is revealed. The research is founded on the stories of women returning to education later in life. The research thus requires a degree of trust between the researcher and the interviewee. The depth of research information declared and revealed by these women to the researcher is a key issue for discussion. Anonymity, gender and context are also discussed at length.

A particularly significant question is then asked relating to depth versus shallow response communication:

Would this issue of identity be revealed through the use of a simple research questionnaire?

Further exploration can then look at a selection of the following issues:

- empowerment of the oppressed;
- inequality;
- collaboration/interaction;
- challenge to dominant ideology;
- role of the researcher in the research process;
- subjectivity;
- reflexive;
- inductive approach;
- theory grounded in the data collected;
- focus on contextual factors;
- power structures;
- research leading to change;
- challenge to dominant ideologies/thinking;
- disadvantage/inequality;
- revelation of 'real' truths;
- action;
- awareness raising;
- revelation of inequality;
- radical thinking;

- challenging existing models;
- centrality of values;
- challenging existing values and systems.

Finally people are asked to consider their own chosen research topic and to look back at the research words used in this session and apply the appropriate language to their own research. This is done in pairs, each sharing thoughts with the other about their research ideas.

Resources required

- A variety of research texts.
- Research glossaries found in the textbooks.
- Masking tape.
- Blank cards.
- Cards with words printed on from Table 5.2 and the list above.
- Empty video boxes or similar.

Tips

In work with trainers in the NHS I have witnessed some excellent experiential learning approaches to clinical research training. One trainer used the statement that there is 'a glass and a half of milk in every bar of chocolate'. The glass and a half was questioned, as was the question of what kind of milk it referred to. Thus the session explored the development of critical questioning required for researchers. Another session used digitized recorded voices of interviews with people about a research area. These voices were then transcribed – indeed, with voice recognition software these voices can be transcribed live with the learners. The voices create words, and these are of course separated from the actual person so that patterns can be detected more easily. The participants can look for patterns together, highlighting them and then coding them together so that it can be recognized that people often see different things in the data. There are multiple interpretations. These learning experiences make the subject of research engaging.

An alternative is to use the research question of whether age affects student performance in learners at university. This is a PhD research subject referred to in a book by Judith Bell, called *Doing Your Research Project*. It can also be used as additional material for this experiential session.

Literature reviewing

This is approached as a three-stage stepped journey.

The first experience involves a simulation using a low level of reality in that it uses a newspaper story for skills awareness and development.

The second experience uses a critical analysis of the skills of literature reviewing, using study skills texts.

The third experience is a critical analysis of journal articles.

Finally, a skills checklist is developed and published by those involved in the experience.

 **References**

Bell, J (1999) *Doing your Research Project*, 3rd edn, Open University Press, Buckingham

Blaxter, L, Hughes, C and Tight, M (1996) *How to Research*, Open University Press, Buckingham

Gill, J and Johnson, P (1991) *Research Methods for Managers*, Paul Chapman Publishing, London

Margerison, C (1988) *Managerial Consulting Skills – A Practical Guide*, Gower, London

Parr, J (2000) *Identity and Education: The Links for Mature Women Students*, Ashgate, Aldershot

Thorpe, R and Moscarola, J (1991) Detecting your research strategy, *Management Education and Development*, **22** (2), pp 127–33

Walk the talk: learning to understand complexity

What it achieves

A kinaesthetic (bodily) approach to learning embeds potentially complex information more deeply in the memory (motor) through a spatial-relational
awareness. Learners research material, construct a lineage, map the facts,
interpret events and walk and talk aloud the learning.

In order to illustrate this experiential approach, the development and
evolution of the environmental movement in Britain will be used. However,
this approach lends itself to any learning and involves complex sequences, a
chronological lineage, that require a spatial-relational understanding. The
history of philosophy or key case material in law are classic examples.

Learning complex subjects by reading textbooks alone often leads to a
struggle to position events, people, time and place in a spatial-chronological
relationship within the human mind. At times the turning of book pages, and
the scrolling of computer screens to absorb and understand complex situations can present barriers to human cognition. This experience uses space,
bodily awareness, conversation and sensory colour coding – to name but a few
of the range of experiential components that aid the process of learning.

Without doubt, 'the environmental story is one of the most complicated and
pressing stories of our time. It involves abstract and probabilistic science, laby-
rinthine laws, grandstanding politicians, speculative economics, and the
complex interplay of individuals and societies'. This quotation is taken from
Stocking, H and Leonard, J P (1990) in a book called *The Greening of the Media*
(Columbia Journalism Review, December, 37–44: 42). It confirms the considerable academic complexity that underlies the evolution of a global social
movement. That is why it is chosen to illustrate this experiential approach.

Underlying principles

Here the concept of 'let the learners do the work' is applied to the design and delivery. The learners are not simply consumers; they are also significant producers of information and interpretation, of materials and tentative theorizing.

The notion of a learning 'journey' underpins this learning activity. The technique explained in detail here uses the learning of a complex history of one of the largest social movements in the world, namely the environmental movement. It is illustrative only and many adaptations can be applied to this technique (see Tips on page 230).

Spatial mapping occurs here in several dimensions: the laws involved, the voluntary and statutory organizations involved and the special designated sites that are themselves created by laws. To this we can add significant people and significant publications such as Darwin's *On the Origin of Species by Means of Natural Selection* or *Blueprint for Survival* or *Silent Spring*.

The activity eventually utilizes space (on the floor or large table) in a creative way, generating multi-dimensional time lines.

This technique also uses learner collaboration and learners as researchers and producers of learning materials.

Colour coding enhances the sensory reception (coloured cards = themes), and the work is supported by a complex electronic database generated by many learners over a period of 20 or more years. This is in itself a useful principle to adopt in the notion of letting the learners do the work as here course materials are continuously created and added to each year by the learners themselves, including booklets and factsheets on the voluntary sector, the laws, the key environmental people, the quangos, significant publications, etc.

Testing/assessment can be added if needed.

With this experience there can be many routes and thus differing stories and interpretations, all derived from this skeletal history of 'facts'.

How to run it

This activity uses learning space in a creative way to 'teach' complex material. The start point for this specific illustrative activity is a brief analysis of the historical database looking for any basic trends that can easily be identified (350-year database of environmental facts and figures – see the book website). This brief start point analysis is completed in groups.

Each group is then assigned specific research themes (laws, voluntary sector, designated land, government organizations). The database is then explored for specific and more detailed trends.

Asking research questions forms the basis of the group investigations:

● When were most voluntary organizations formed?
● What kind or type of organizations are they?
● How have they changed over the years?
● How have campaign tactics changed?

This starts the journey of analysis. Other groups will explore the laws, the quangos, the designated sites, etc.

In higher-education applications, learners might be asked each week to contribute to the development of materials. This might attract 10 per cent of the marks: eg a voluntary organization factsheet exploring areas identified by the learners, such as when the organizations were formed, what their objectives are, how many members they have, etc. If one person hands in a factsheet, they may get 50 or so back in return depending on the size of the group! This is the collaborative principle. All the factsheets are copied and bound into a booklet for further investigation, and returned to learners.

Several booklets can be built up over a number of years. They act as reference documents for further analysis. In addition, lectures and seminars can be given on any of these themes over the weeks.

In the final analysis, students are asked to use all the resources developed to create a spatial-relational map using the whole set of coloured cards, with one end of the room representing the year 1600, and the other end representing the present day. Additional blank cards can be given out to fill in. But participants do this only for their own specific research area.

The journey focus will vary in each group, but a talk will be given by each research team. The composite talk of their walk must include everyone in the group, and it must explore the complex spatial-relational nature of events in the history of environmentalism.

Each walking journey will be recorded and marks allocated at a later date. By digitally recording the Walk the talk by individuals who have been allocated specific research themes, a digital database is also created. The digital recordings can be given to the learners to edit using free software such as Audacity (available on the web).

Walking and talking and sharing in this way, the experience can reduce the stress that is found in many other forms of assessment: learning and assessment appear to the learner to seamlessly merge into each other.

The picture-map layout on the floor or table demonstrates their knowledge of the subject and when it is finished, students walk the talk, presenting the historical picture as they proceed. This kinaesthetically reinforces the learning and tests understanding in a visual-oral way.

Participants eventually take over and become architects of what is now their own learning space.

Outline of possible instructions for learners

The following represents just one idea for using the database:

1. Split into small groups.
2. Each group must take on the exploration of one theme selected from a total of five research themes: laws, voluntary organizations, designated sites, key events, government organizations.
3. Using a highlighter, select all the most interesting and relevant facts and figures in your theme, using the database.
4. Develop a brief analysis and commentary on the trends that you have observed.
5. Having developed some expertise in your theme area, work collaboratively with the other groups to lay out the cards on the floor or on a large boardroom-style table. Using one end as the year 1600 and the other as today, map out the history of environmentalism. Blank cards can be used to add to the timeline.
6. When you are ready, take the tutor through the history by all walking the talk together.
7. Write up brief notes for the development of an assignment.

 **Resources required**

● Empty video box (all the essential kit and instructions for learners can, for example, be presented in a plastic video case).
● Instructions and front sheet design to be inserted into the video-box sleeve.
● Coloured laminated cards with key information on with dates.
● Database booklet.

The five themes are:

1. voluntary organizations;
2. designated sites;
3. major laws (such as the National Parks Act);

4. quangos

5. major events in history.

The colour coding is as follows:

1. yellow – for voluntary organizations;

2. green – for designated sites;

3. blue – for major laws;

4. grey – for quangos;

5. orange – for major events in history.

Coloured cards, with key information on, might include any of the material from the database, such as:

- Yellow:
    - Conservation Corps/BTCV – 1959;
    - Greenpeace – 1971;
    - Groundwork – 1981;
    - Friends of the Earth – 1970;
    - Earthfirst! – 1988;
    - RSPB – 1891;
    - National Trust – 1895;
    - Ramblers Association – 1935;
    - World Wide Fund For Nature – 1961.
- Green:
    - National Parks;
    - Areas of Outstanding Natural Beauty – first designated in 1957;
    - Local Nature Reserves – first in Scotland in 1951;
    - Country Parks – first established in 1969;
    - Marine Nature Reserves – first in 1986.
- Blue:
    - 1949 National Parks and Access to the Countryside Act;
    - 1981 Wildlife and Countryside Act;
    - 1968 Countryside Act;
    - 1995 Environment Act.
- Grey:
    - Countryside Agency;
    - Natural England;
    - Countryside Council for Wales;
    - Environment Agency.

● Orange:
  – World Wars;
  – Mass trespass.

Tips

Further development ideas: other coloured cards can be designed for major outbreaks of illnesses and diseases, eg Black Death, smog, foot and mouth, bird flu.

Laminated pictures of key texts such as *Silent Spring* (Rachel Carson), *Small is Beautiful* (Michael Shumacher) and *Blueprint for Survival*.

Small sequences of cards can be built initially to show connections or trends or chronological developments. Try using, for example, 10 voluntary-sector cards on their own so as to see trends. Then select 10 designated-site cards to place on the floor. The whole picture might be built over a long period of time.

Other applications

This technique can be used for any historical event, the history of computers, the history of mobile phones, the history of philosophy, corporate company history, complex sequential financial work such as an invoicing and claims system – any context where the routes are complex and not easily remembered or understood.

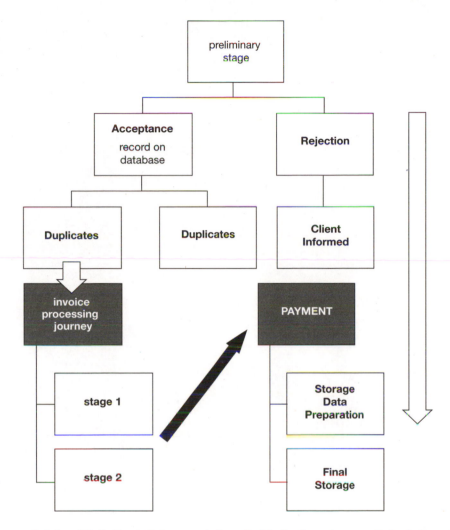

Figure 5.5.1   *Walk the talk is especially suitable for learning spatial-relational complexity such as in financial systems*

Part 6

The sixth dimension: being

Introduction

Focus

- Understanding the practical issues that underlie personal change.
- The important practice question here is: What is it that encourages people to change the 'self'?

What is it that gives us the will to learn, to change and do things differently? The link between learning and change often becomes apparent only when we consider both elements more closely. An observation by Charles Handy in *The Age of Unreason* (1989) brings the two more closely together:

> If changing is, as I have argued, only another word for learning, the theories of learning will also be the theories of changing. Those who are always learning are those who can ride the waves of change and who see a changing world as full of opportunities rather than of damage. They are the ones most likely to be the survivors in a time of discontinuity. They are also the enthusiasts and the architects of new ways and forms and ideas. If you want to change, try learning, one might say or, more precisely, if you want to be in control of your change, take learning more seriously.

Trying too hard?

The Inner Game of Tennis by Timothy Gallwey (1986), a tennis coach and former junior tennis champion in the United States, has become a classic. Through the medium of tennis, Gallwey has made a number of observations about the nature of learning and experiencing. His first observation was that the secret of winning a game of tennis was not to try too hard, with the result that the mind became more relaxed and it became easier to make better shots. As a new coach he had also noticed some apparent anomalies when he tried to coach some pupils. Namely, some of the errors his pupils made seemed to correct themselves without his intervention or the pupils being aware of the improvement. Gallwey was also conscious of sometimes overteaching his pupils and the fact that on occasions his attempts to improve a particular stroke resulted in a deteriorating performance from the pupil. Telling pupils to lift their shoulder might result in other errors creeping into their game, with the result that they concentrated even more, causing further deterioration. Gallwey theorized that there would appear to be two elements of the self involved with the game of tennis or other activities, ie the conscious self and the unconscious self. Self 1 is the part of the brain that is the conscious teller, which instructs the body and says such things as, 'Keep the racquet head closer to the ground in order to give the ball more topspin.' Self 2, the unconscious automatic doer, carries out the various movements needed to play a game of tennis.

Being in the world

It is easy to neglect or disown this part of ourselves, this inner self. Over-concentration on knowledge as how we 'know' the world can lead to being-apart-from-the-world as opposed to being-in-the-world. Howard Gardner (1993) commented that the 'sense of self' placed most strain on his multiple intelligence theory: the self goes beyond intelligence. Appreciating the wholeness of the experience of learning can connect everyday knowing with the more abstract theoretical understanding. Experiential learning is not solely concerned with experience of everyday events or forms of knowing about the world. Experiential learning can engage us at a much deeper level, connecting to our spiritual self, our values and our ethically driven self that is also located in the unconscious that is our being (the ontological self). The whole experience of learning is a connectedness of the outer being with the inner being, the conscious with the subconscious. There is no clear separation between the outer and inner self. Edward Cell (1984: 9) remarked that: 'In learning to live with less self-awareness, we also diminish those distinctively human possibilities for freedom, creativity, caring, and ethical insight which are based on that awareness.' Cell devoted a whole chapter to 'Learning and the struggle to be'. He noted (1984: 9) that 'Our sense of worth becomes less and less tied to having approval from others and more and more grounded in knowing ourselves to be the creators of meaning and value.' Experiential learning should ideally intensify our sense of freedom and liberate our creative potential.

In exploring our own behaviours, as they relate to our deeper inner self, sometimes an uncomfortable 'shadow side' of the self is revealed. This often reveals how much we divert conscious attention by being occupied with having, getting, wanting, knowing and doing. To acknowledge and work with this shadow side can lead to greater wisdom. In the spirit of service to others, 'service learning' is an activity covered in this section: it is not about taking or getting, or learning from doing, but about learning from giving.

Scope of Part 6

Five main activities are presented in Part 6. In order to gain a more complete understanding of the being dimension, all five illustrative experiences are briefly explained below. Experience 1.5: Listening to silence (on page 73) is also a very good exercise exercise that can be added to Part 6.

✔ Experience 6.1: Cards on the table

This experience involves raising self-awareness by playing cards. It is a fun way to learn about ourselves, involving both individual and group assessment. The relaxed playing of cards is an essential ambient backcloth to this experiential exploration, involving personal portrayals, action planning, commitment to personal change and the discovery of 'shadow sides'.

✔ Experience 6.2: Comic strips and newspapers

This experience involves the development of reflective storylines using popular media such as a newspaper design or comic strips as a template. The personal and group reflective stories about experiences can include both visual and audio storylines. Speech-capture software can be used for voiceover work.

✔ Experience 6.3: Behavioural awareness

Individual behavioural awareness and sensitization to improved communicative options lead to personal change in communication patterns when we are involved in group interaction.

✓ *Experience 6.4: Service learning*

Service learning supports and gives, for example, time, commitment and expertise to individuals, community or environmental initiatives. Learning from individual or corporate giving is certainly a different learning experience.

✓ *Experience 6.5: Unmasking*

Unmasking is an experience that can reveal interesting sides to our 'self'. Could we see ourselves in a different light? Should we ask our colleagues how they see us? Creating and playing with masks as different personas can also be entertaining.

A range of other concepts to work on in the being dimension

1. Working with self-awareness.
2. Managing transfer and reflective practice.
3. Working with the unconscious competence.
4. Planning to learn and working with emergent opportunities.
5. Seeking transformational experiences but remaining open to emerging opportunities.
6. Developing authenticity, autonomy and interdependence.
7. Becoming aware of your sense of identity; I am... exercises are good for this: ask yourself what is important in your life.
8. Developing an understanding of the bigger picture in life.
9. Dwelling in nature and feeling and sensing being alone with yourself.
10. Cultivating meditative spaces.
11. Cultivating life balance: an important theme; mind–body; emotion–reason; developing the mind–body, affect–reason balance and allowing regular times to work with these aspects of yourself.
12. Protecting some blank, quiet space to 'think' each day, each week.
13. Jogging, ironing, plodding the hills, swimming the lengths, mowing lawns, driving regular routes – all present opportunities for reflective-meditative states of mind, being rhythmic, repetitive and typically involving relatively mindless physical exercise.

14. Developing general expressive skills of writing, such as autobiographies, and continuous awareness; speech-recognition software can be very powerful; completing here-and-now unfinished statements – for example: 'Right now I am aware of…'.

 **References**

Cell, E (1984) *Learning to Learn from Experience*, State University of New York Press, Albany, USA

Gallwey, T (1986) *The Inner Game of Tennis*, Pan Books, London

Gardner, H (1993) *Frames of Mind: The Theory of Multiple Intelligences*, 2nd edn, Basic Books, New York

Handy, C (1989) *The Age of Unreason*, Business Books, London

Cards on the table: learning to change by playing cards

What it achieves

This experience involves individual and group self-assessment, action planning and personal change.

This occurs through the experience of playing cards.

Underlying principles

Questionnaires are perceived as 'done on you' and they can get rather tedious to fill in and they often do not get people to fully engage with the subject. Some learners often reject the findings. However, most questionnaires can be turned into a more engaging card game.

Playing cards are designed and used in this technique to improve self-reflection, action planning and change. The activity also develops a decision-making process called 'The interview' to explore existing group dynamics and individual strengths and weaknesses.

This session requires learners to make their own choices about statements that best describe themselves, as found on playing cards. The session is set in a relaxed environment (can be experienced with drinks and biscuits or snack food available, with background music playing quietly).

The first phase of the card exercise involves a self-assessment.

The second phase involves a participative enquiry and group analysis.

The third phase involves identifying the characteristics of a new team member, using the requirement of an interview for someone to be recruited to join the existing team.

Finally, each learner develops an action plan for their personal change.

How to run it

Design a range of 'I am...' statements such as:

- I am a good listener.
- I am impatient of poor work.
- I can be over sensitive.
- I am a workaholic.
- I make sure projects meet deadlines.

These can be acquired by exploring a range of team, group-dynamic and psychological profiling-type questionnaires and selecting statements that are suitable from each. The statements are put on laminated cards or they can be produced professionally by card manufacturers.

Duplicate sets are required of these cards so that there are copies for a few groups to play as required. The statements also need to be duplicated two or three times within the pack so that more than one person can choose any particular statement. However, it is not essential that people always pick the card they wish to have, as they can write cards they have seen and not been able to acquire, and the purpose of the activity is to generate self-profiling, group discussion and plans for self-change.

Further examples of individual or team statement cards could include:

- I am hard headed and unemotional.
- I am communicative and outgoing.
- I am a good listener.
- I am prepared to take risks.
- I have a tendency to be stubborn or oppositional.
- I need to know the rules and boundaries.
- I am very creative.
- I have an emotional guardedness.
- I have a strong devotion to work.

- I am good at report writing.
- I am very logical and love problem solving and crosswords.

Cards might include statements about team dynamics or team stages criteria, such as:

- I am a good team player.
- I am a people motivator.
- I am happiest when working on projects.
- I prefer to lead and chair things.
- I am good at bringing people together.
- I like to resolve conflict.
- I am good at evaluating ideas and projects.

Cards might include statements about learning styles and learning skills, such as:

- I like to learn from books.
- I enjoy communicating by letter.
- Speaking aloud is one of my strengths.
- I am good at making compelling arguments.
- I am comfortable with working out compromises.
- I have a good memory.
- Even when I'm upset about something I can generally ignore this and put it to one side.
- I learn quite well from lectures.
- I prefer hands-on seminars that let you do things.
- I work well with diagrams.

Rules of the game

You can develop your own card-game rules. For example, rummy-style rules can be used. Here you deal five or six cards to each person (any more than this cannot easily be held in the hand). The central idea is for each learner to end up with a hand that best describes them. However, any cards that are seen that the player likes as a statement that does apply to them can be written down by them on the action plan form shown in Table 6.1.1. The learners play by either picking up a blind card or the 'seen' card put down by the previous

Figure 6.1.1   *Learning and change by playing cards (oil company staff, India)*

player. One card then has to be returned to the pack on the table, so keeping a hand of five cards. After reflecting and playing all the cards, the players then put their cards face up on the table and discuss what they have, and share information. They thus get to know the team profile better and are eventually asked to develop a personal and/or team strengths and limitations sheet.

 **Resources required**

- Questionnaire converted into cards.
- Set of game rules.
- Interpretation sheets.
- Handout sheets (examples provided in Tables 6.1.1 and 6.1.2).

Tips

As variations, tutors can add to card descriptors, create whole new packs or ask the learners to create other traits or personality descriptors.

Cards can be professionally made when they have been tested and proved to be satisfactory. Card statements need to be printed at the top and the bottom of the cards, facing both up and down so that they can be read by people all round the table.

Table 6.1.1   *Example of an individual action plan sheet*

My cards	
My top five statements	Additional card statements
A characteristic I would love to have but it just isn't me!	
My action plan	

Table 6.1.2   *Example of a group action plan sheet*

My cards	
Our group strengths	Our group weaknesses
Characteristics or traits we need in our group	

Comic strips and newspapers: reflection and change using storylines

What it achieves

The experience involves the creation of popular news media, such as a newspaper or comic strips, to generate personal and group learning. The change is driven by guided reflection upon experiences that are relived and told in digital or written storytelling linked to visual images.

Underlying principles

This session uses visual digital images, narrative creation and collaborative media-production processes to develop a powerful reflective experience. The images help retrieval of the contextual setting and specific scenarios of learning. It is a good activity for anchoring thoughts and feelings about organizational and individual change in a non-threatening way.

Edward Cell in *Learning to Learn from Experience* (1984) notes that T S Eliot 'has suggested that experience is like a partially developed roll of film. As we later reflect on it, especially as we look back from a new perspective, we may develop it further, bringing out more of its meaning'. This is the basis of this experiential activity.

How to run it

Comic strips

Learners are asked to take many digital photographs (many people have such a capability on mobile phones) during specific experiences or events over a period of time (training course, event, programme, contract delivery, product design experiences, a semester at university.

At the end of this period, ask participants to select a specific number of images, say six, and, using speech and thought bubbles on PowerPoint® (click on Insert, Shapes, Callouts, and Speech and thought bubbles will appear at the base), they are asked to download these images and then develop a narrative consisting of thoughts and feelings about learning and change in themselves either as individuals or in small groups.

If deeper reflection is required (and less humorous), then move from a comic-strip to a newspaper, biography or other more serious format. I have also used an epitaph approach! This activity can also be used for personal and professional development activities, such as creation of personal web or portfolio profiles. Make a point of addressing this need to be funny in using comic

Figure 6.2.1   *Comic strips and newspapers: add speech and thought bubbles to photographs*

strips: it is not necessary. The story might have a character, a villain, a central theme and a punchline. People want to enjoy the experience of collaboratively deciding the story parameters.

The emphasis is on the detail of the narrative. Using speakers and microphones and a free recording and simple editing software called Audacity, a digital voiceover narrative can also be created alongside the visual images.

This exercise can follow on from other experiences in this book such as Ace of spades (Chapter 4.1) or String lines (Chapter 4.5), exploring the feeling dimension.

Newspapers

This session has also been used for corporate conferences, where an early-morning conference 'newspaper' was produced by attendees. The morning paper offered a wide range of reflective formats, headline stories and visual images. This experience is well suited to a range of experiences, and also lends itself well to active subjects such as outdoor management development or adventure education.

Rules, restrictions or time limits can be added to the experience; for example:

- The story could include themes such as creativity leadership or decision making.
- The main learning points should be encapsulated within the storyline.
- The story must cover all the characters and include themes about 1) the most exciting times; 2) the funniest times; 3) the boring times; and 4) the greatest learning times.

 **Resources required**

- Digital camera, assorted pictures of participants completing activities over any period of time.
- Computer with PowerPoint® or similar programme, and Audacity editing and recording software or similar programme.

Tips

This exercise can also be done with ordinary photographs using large sheets or in a scrap book so that the storyline can be written.

It can be done with ordinary photo slides on a projector, with learners developing a verbal storyline and reading it out as the slides are being shown.

It can be used for creative story writing.

It can be done as a group wiki with a template.

It can be useful for reflecting on a learning journey over time.

 **References and further reading**

Beard, C and Rhodes, T (2002) Experiential learning: using comic strips as 'reflective tools' in adult learning, *Australian Journal of Outdoor Education*, **6** (2), 58–65

Cell, E (1984) *Learning to Learn from Experience*, State University of New York Press, Albany

Good examples of digital stories can be viewed on http://www.bbc.co.uk/capturewales/

Behavioural awareness: changing individual and group behavioural interactions

What it achieves

This experience explores individual and group behavioural awareness and sensitization, leading to personal change in communication patterns involving group interaction.

Underlying principles

In traditional behaviour analysis work, trained experts watch a group interact. They carry out an analysis and then inform individuals and groups of the results. In this experiential activity the learners take overall responsibility for the process of awareness and change. The suggested experiences outlined below can work on change in a creative way. Creative options, choice and ownership are the central principles for this learner-centred approach.

How to run it

Below is a list of the basic behaviours that can also be used in intervention skills in facilitation or process observation, therapy, coaching and consultation. If you want to learn more, relevant books are listed at the end of this experiential activity.

Behavioural specialists can set up experiences whereby participants express their ideas, beliefs and attitudes. When awareness is heightened, in terms of behavioural dynamics, there is a greater sensitivity to the behaviours exhibited by themselves and others, an improvement in listening skills, a greater degree of openness, and an increased tolerance of individual differences.

John Heron has also written extensively on facilitation skills and facilitator interventions. *Helping the Client* (1990) offers a range of interventions and interactions, including: echoing, selective echoing, open and closed questioning, empathetic divining, checking understanding, paraphrasing, logical marshalling, following, consulting, proposing or leading, bringing in and shutting out.

To take selective echoing as an example, this 'involves the facilitator in selecting some word or phrase that carries an emotional charge or stands out as significant in its context' (Heron, 1990: 266). This is done in order to give the client space to explore, in any direction, the significance of that which has been reflected or echoed back to them. This kind of intervention involves a degree of selective interpretation without leading the story and it can help the client to focus.

These intervention and interaction skills are basic interpersonal skills, and they are applied and developed extensively in the helping professions; they also form the essence of good facilitation. In therapeutic work McLeod (1997), in *Narrative and Psychotherapy*, similarly offers a list of intervention and interaction skills:

- Approval. Provides emotional support, approval, reassurance, or reinforcement. Accepting or validating the client's story.
- Information. Supplies information in the form of data, facts or resources. It may be related to the therapy process, the therapist's behaviour or therapy arrangements (time, place).
- Direct guidance. These are directions or advice that the therapist suggests for the client, either for what to do in the session or outside the session. Structuring the process of storytelling.
- Closed question. Gathers data or specific information. The client responses are limited and specific. Filling in the story.

- Open question. Probes for or requests clarification or exploration by the client. From a narrative perspective, open questioning can be used to invite the telling of a story or to explore the meaning of elements of a story.

- Paraphrase. Mirrors or summarizes what the client has been communicating either verbally or non-verbally. Does not 'go beyond' what the client has said or add a new perspective or understanding to the client's statements or provide any explanation for the client's behaviour. Includes restatement of content, reflection of feelings, non-verbal reference and summary. Therapists using a narrative approach may wish to communicate to the client that they have 'heard' the story, or may attempt to focus attention on a particular aspect of a story.

- Interpretation. Goes beyond what the client has overtly recognized and provides reasons, alternative meanings or new frameworks for feelings, behaviours or personality. It may establish connections between seemingly isolated statements or events; interpret defences, feelings of resistance, or transference; or indicate themes, patterns or causal relationships in behaviour and personality, relating present events to past events. This response includes a wide range of narrative-informed interventions, centred on the general goal of retelling the story in different ways.

- Confrontation. Points out a discrepancy or contradiction but does not provide a reason for such a discrepancy. This discrepancy may be between words and behaviours, between two things a client has said, or between the client's and the therapist's perceptions. In narrative therapy, the client is encouraged to resolve the tension or incongruity between opposing versions of a story.

- Self-disclosure. Shares feelings or personal experiences. The therapist gives an account of his or her own story, either in terms of relevant episodes from a personal life story, or framed in terms of a therapeutic meta-narrative, or drawn from a myth and other cultural sources.

McLeod, 1997: 114

These essential skills are also very similar to the behaviours identified by the Huthwaite Group (Rackham and Morgan, 1977) and they are used in what they term 'behaviour analysis work'. They include proposing, building, supporting, disagreeing, defending/attacking, testing understanding, summarizing, seeking information, giving information, bringing in, shutting out.

In checking understanding, for example, the facilitation phrase might be 'So can I just check this. What you are saying is...?' This gentle checking intervention encourages and checks the story, rather than redirecting it.

The use of these skills is also discussed in *The Facilitator's Toolkit* by Maggie Havergal and John Edmonstone (2003: 110). Good communication and interaction require the development of these skills.

In the experiences below I am going to break these skills down by introducing the simple concept of dividing them into pushing behaviours and pulling behaviours. Some do not fit easily within these two categories:

- Pushing
  - Giving information – offering facts, opinions or clarification.
  - Disagreeing – explicit direct and reasoned declaration of a difference of opinion or which criticizes another person's opinion or concept.
  - Defending/attacking – attacking another person or defensively strengthening own position, often with emotional undertones.
  - Blocking/difficulty stating – putting a block in the path of others such as 'It can't be done… it's not that simple'.
  - Open – open admission of mistakes or inadequacies of arguments; exposes person, who therefore can be open to ridicule or loss of status.
- Pulling
  - Proposing – suggests or puts forward a new concept or course of action.
  - Building – extends or develops a proposal.
  - Supporting – explicit declaration of support of or agreement with a person or their concepts.
  - Testing understanding – establishing whether or not a contribution has been understood.
  - Seeking information – facts, opinions or clarification.
  - Summarizing – summarizes or restates in a compact form previous items/issues/concepts.

When working with groups it is important to identify which of these skills we use, which of them more of and which of them fewer of, when and under what circumstances. Meetings, for example, might move to predominantly pulling behaviours towards the second half of the time allocation. Information giving and seeking will occur at the early stages of a meeting. We might want to balance advocacy and critical inquiry, for example, in certain circumstances.

In the experiential learning approaches suggested below I advocate that people use behavioural statement cards to develop group and self-awareness.

The cards can be used for whole groups in a meeting or for individuals. They can simply be laid out or used actively by playing them when speaking – eventually they become automatically part of our self-awareness.

The number of cards in a pile next to the person represents the number of times they speak – 'air time' – and who is speaking most and least. The kind of cards used reveals repertoire bias – indicating a need for change. In a good meeting the cards differ between the first half and the second half: this is important.

This behavioural analysis can also be used in the form of a job-selection grid in recruitment exercises where participants are asked to collectively debate discussion topics.

Cards (with the texts shown below) are spread out in front of a group of learners. They are given time to look at the categories, which are all explained by the trainer (in addition, the details are printed on the backs of the cards).

Option 1

The learners look at the cards, and then answer a set of four questions:

1. What behaviours most commonly surface and are seen in your meetings at work?
2. What are your own most common behaviours, ie what do you do more of and what do you do less of?
3. Do you think the pattern of these meetings might be changed for the better?
4. Are there changes that you could make to improve your own contributions to meetings?

A discussion of these issues then follows.

Option 2

To sensitize participants to their own behaviour, each person has a set of cards spread out directly in front of them. A conversation is started about a controversial issue, that will trigger individual values being expressed. Each time a person speaks, the category of behaviour is mentally noted by that person or briefly touched during or after speaking. These are options to try out. At the end of the session each person must note how much air time they took up, ie how many times they spoke, and what categories were more frequent or less frequent. The issue of category appropriateness is also worth considering.

Option 3

Arrange the cards on a large table in terms of the behaviours seen in a typical meeting structure, with one end of the table the start of the meeting and the other as the end of the meeting. The result is invariably a discussion of the obvious diamond shape of meetings, that is, meetings first open out, and at the end they close down.

The behaviours associated with the beginning, middle and end of meetings are then spread out.

A discussion of these issues then follows.

All three options can be used in combination.

It is important to develop a plan for change, and to find regular opportunities to practise.

Resources required

Large laminated cards with the following interaction behaviours written in large print:

- proposing;
- building on other ideas;
- information giving;
- supporting;
- approval;
- direct guidance;
- confronting;
- disagreeing;
- attacking;
- defending;
- testing understanding;
- summarizing;
- seeking clarification;
- bringing in people;
- blocking people out;
- self-disclosure.

Full definitions can be written on the rear of the cards for clarification.

Tips

Three ideas for behavioural awareness practice:

1. Take a short piece of video (TV soap?) and analyse the conversation using the behavioural repertoire grid.

2. Next time you make a complaint on the phone, record your conversations using a hands-free phone and a digital recorder, and play back the conversation; check your professional practice skills.

3. The cards or a checklist can be carried round by individuals for personal use in meetings and other business interactions for increased practice, sensitization and change.

References and further reading

Beard, C and Wilson, J (2006) *Experiential Learning: A Best Practice Handbook for Educators and Trainers*, Kogan Page, London

Egan, G (2002) *The Skilled Helper*, Brooks/Cole Publishing, Pacific Grove CA

Havergal, M and Edmonstone, J (2003) *The Facilitator's Toolkit*, 2nd edn, Gower, Aldershot

Heron, J (1990) *Helping the Client: a creative practical guide*, Sage, London

McLeod, J (1997) *Narrative and Psychotherapy*, Sage, London

Rackham, N and Morgan, T (1977) *Behaviour Analysis in Training*, McGraw-Hill, London

Service learning: social and environmental responsibility

What it achieves

Service learning adopts the principle of making a positive contribution to the service of the community or to the environment, while simultaneously experiencing a powerful learning activity that motivates and engages with the sense of giving and responsibility to others.

This experience is illustratively included in the being dimension as it involves learning by giving rather than doing and by not getting but giving – of the self rather than for the self.

Social and environmental responsibility

This kind of service undertaking can be used as a substitute for typical team-building exercises, which involve surfacing issues related to, say, group interaction, group power or leadership activities. Such a typical activity in the outdoors traditionally involved the building of a raft using planks and drums and rope. While such an activity can be great fun, it has no real output in relation to the energy expended and the merchandise developed. This is also the case with the Bike it! experience in the doing section of this book (see Chapter 2.1).

Underlying principles

This session introduces the real projects that have a positive output in terms of a benefit to the environment or society. It is about giving.

The service element seems to produce a heightened, sometimes powerful, learning experience, and it also can be a productive way to increase environmental awareness in people (see Beard, 1996).

Learner-centred choice is usually built into these projects, with social and environmental decision making, and with personal responsibility and active engagement very much part of the learning experience.

How to run it

Many organizations are now substituting environmental activities or community-based activities in place of recreation pursuits such as raft building, climbing or abseiling. One leading supermarket chain, for example, made the following remark to me back in the 1980s: 'Colin, we've spent many years now doing the usual outdoor stuff. It's got to a point where our managers can be on one mountain waving to our competitors on another mountain doing exactly the same thing. We need something different. Everyone seems to have done the rafts, planks and drums bit. We need something different to develop our staff: something more engaging and real.'

What was asked for in this case were programmes that were much more real and more empathetic to the experience of the natural environment. Battling with the elements had become the tradition and it was time for a change. Many training or human resource development managers now work more closely, for example, with national parks and voluntary organizations to plan environmental or community projects for experiential learning events.

In this way experiential programmes can have double value: a real purposeful learning outcome and a constructive application of human energy from people contributing. Such productive engagement is more satisfying than simply packing away all the drums and planks at the end of simulated activities, to await their reuse by the next set of participants.

Significantly, real projects seem to have a positive motivational impact on client learning, affecting the way participants engage in learning from experience. Such projects are perceived as doing good work, of a charitable nature, of giving 'service'. My belief is that the high emotional response to such an experience leads to high-quality learning experiences. This phenomenon still requires more research, but the reconnection with the community and the Earth appears to be of value. This speculative benefit of using natural environments to create natural thinking has a lot more development potential for the future of working practices.

Popular community projects include:

- building playgrounds for children;
- designing and delivering hospital radio programmes;
- theatre performances;
- building structures on public footpaths, such as walkway bridges over streams;
- dry stone walling, tree planting or pond clearance.

The options are indeed endless and with creativity the benefits can be considerable to all parties concerned.

Longstanding charitable organizations such as the Royal Society for the Protection of Birds (RSPB) and the National Trust in the UK offer such team challenges in their volunteer-work brochures, and have specialist staff to help to coordinate such projects. The BTCV also has many such projects available across Europe.

The tasks that require completion for charities include working on their land, which can be entrusted stately homes or important reserves for nature. The charities outline projects that are particularly suitable for corporate management development projects. This aligns with contemporary ideas that develop further the notion of corporate social responsibility, social accountability, social auditing and the notion of business as a positive social force (in the UK the Institute of Social and Ethical Accountability was formed in 1996). These social and environmental activities are popular and an increasing number of people are willing to travel from and to overseas destinations to help with this kind of work.

To cite a specific case example, one very large surveying and mapping organization asked me for help in designing such a project to replace the usual outdoor-pursuit events that they had run for many years. I contacted people in the RSPB, the National Trust, the BTCV, the Wildlife Trusts and the National Parks and asked them all to send me a two-page outline of what they could do with 30 experienced surveyors over a two-day event, detailing clearly the benefits to wildlife. All of them responded with details of the beneficial projects.

The client organization then had to choose the ideal project for them to carry out and all the other participating organizations were notified of the decision and thanked for their efforts. Those that were not successful at their projects were held in reserve for a later opportunity.

In this instance the RSPB was chosen and the surveyors stayed in a hotel for the event and were briefed by a team of facilitators. Team building lay at the very heart of this event. Time pressures and other challenges were designed into the project. A particularly difficult challenge was the difficult terrain that was to be surveyed. The land had been flooded to different degrees by peat extraction industries. Safety and risk assessment was taken seriously.

The outcome was even more positive than expected:

● The RSPB was amazed at the quality of the new maps developed for this very difficult terrain. The maps enabled the bird-protection work to move ahead in many new ways, with accurate mapping now in place.

● Excellent teamwork skills were developed under the considerable time pressure and a sense of project engagement, commitment and excitement was palpable.

● A new set of ideas for a surveying service was initiated.

 **Resources required**

Contact the appropriate charities for advice and help.

 Tips

Some organizations (eg The Body Shop) have allowed staff specified periods of company time to work with charities (eg for up to one day a month).

See social and environmental charity websites for contacts and for the kind of projects that might be undertaken.

See also edventure in Chapter 1.3 for more ideas.

 **Reference**

Beard, C M (1996) Environmental awareness training – three ideas for change, *Eco-Management and Auditing*, **3** (3), November 1996

Unmasking: the hidden and unknown self

What it achieves

Masks can get into the hidden and unknown aspects of our persona and help to unlock ideas that normally remain hidden in the subconscious.

Working with the right side of the brain, masks provide a vehicle for the expression of new insights about ourselves.

Underlying principles

Masks can help to unlock ideas that normally remain in the subconscious, as the hidden and unknown aspects of the self (see *The Johari Window*, Luft, 1961).

This session considers one of many learning methods that lower dimensions of reality. Working with the so-called real everyday human person as presented to the outside world is not necessarily always the best strategy for experiencing a sense of self. This experience is also kinaesthetic in that it involves making and wearing a mask. The experience also involves feedback from others, which can also help to unlock aspects of our subconscious mind.

How to run it

Blank masks can be purchased as templates for this experience. Face paints can be used as an alternative for the creation of a different self.

Creating masks can accelerate our learning in a number of ways. They can:

- deepen our understanding of ourselves as we surface and explore our unconscious or unacknowledged assumptions, which have been taken for granted;
- focus on the uniqueness of each individual's situation; this is not a simple puzzle with a right answer but a complex issue with a range of possible solutions;
- use metaphor to assist us to identify (or clarify) our sense of self, our strengths and our 'over-strengths';
- access the creative side of our brain, which uses images, shape, colour and takes a holistic view;
- take us beyond aesthetics and art – we are not creating pleasing objects that are gentle to the eye but are identifying strong statements that help us to explore within and express ourselves more fully;
- provide the opportunity to work with others, gain feedback and support and have fun;
- offer a hands-on, kinaesthetic activity.

This kind of work requires careful consideration, so follow the notes provided here carefully. When encouraging participants to wear masks, ask them to turn away from others as they put on their mask and take time to acquaint themselves with the mask they have made. This facilitates the persona of the mask to emerge in the ensuing conversation between two people working together on the event. The process is repeated when they take off the mask – ie they should turn away again.

As well as talking with others about the persona that has emerged, it can also be useful (and often revealing) to get feedback from someone – what do they see in the mask? It can also be useful to see your mask being worn by someone else.

Masks can be part of a process of expressing how we perceive ourselves: maybe as a wise old owl dispensing wisdom. The masks can provide an opportunity for gaining feedback on how you are perceived by others. This kinaesthetic process, involving feedback from others, can also help to unlock aspects of our subconscious mind.

Making masks engages the right side, the creative side, of the brain, using metaphor, symbolism and thinking holistically through imagery. For many people, accelerating learning by using both sides of the brain simultaneously is an unfamiliar and challenging process. Typically, much of our work makes demands on the left side, the logical side, of our brain, which engages in linear processes and language. Working in a kinaesthetic way can stimulate creativity, leading to unexpected insights and 'Ah-ha' moments. These may not emerge through more usual learning processes that rely on only visual or auditory communication.

In experimenting with processes such as mask making on ourselves, we will gain greater insight not only into our own professional practice but also into the processes we might suggest or employ with our learners.

Transforming our masks: transforming ourselves

A powerful use of masks involves transformation of the mask as a metaphor for transforming ourselves. Making new masks of our future self allows us to create a vision of what we might become and how.

Transformation involves:

- letting go of old images and metaphors;
- adding, changing or subtracting some aspect of our beliefs, attitudes or behaviours.

By applying this thinking to the masks, we can either make new masks or transform our existing masks into our future self. Both of these approaches have aspects that commend them. In making new masks, we retain the original representation of some aspect of ourselves that we want to change; in transforming a mask, we (metaphorically) experience the difficulties of changing some aspect of ourselves.

We need both in-depth awareness and skill in facilitation when working with masks as metaphors.

 Resources required

- Blank masks or face paint.

 Tips

When using masks, there are some advantages and potential pitfalls to be aware of:

Advantages:

- accessibility;
- application to real life/work issues;
- flexibility;
- depth;
- can be quick (20–60 minutes);
- challenging – because many participants have primarily cerebral jobs, they find it hard to be involved in a practical, hands on, kinaesthetic task;
- can work for one-to-one situations or with groups;
- enables physical transformation (of mask) as a metaphor for visualizing future behavioural transformation.

Pitfalls:

- care needed with process: important to structure this experience so that appropriate thinking, reflection and feedback time is included;
- care needed as it is easy to go into deep areas of ourselves very quickly;
- needs resources and private space to be messy in;
- can be an advantage to have art/creative training or knowledge;
- challenging (especially to those not used to creative approaches);
- can be perceived to be superficial;
- mask process might get in the way of engaging with issues.

Acknowledgement

This description of the mask experience has been supported by the work of Vivien Whitaker and Toby Rhodes.

 **References and further reading**

Gass, M (1995) *Book of Metaphors Volume II*, Kendall Hunt, Dubuque IA, USA
Goffman, E (1971) *The Presentation of Self in Everyday Life*, Penguin, London
Johnstone, K (1981) *Impro*, Methuen, London
Luft, J (1961) The Johari Window, *Human Training News*, **5** (1)

Index

NB: page numbers in *italic* indicate figures or tables